WEST HEMPSTEAD PUBLIC LIBRARY

3 1855 00072 8279

W9-CNK-353

AUG 1 **5** 1989

J 347.035 B
Bernstein, Richard B.
Into the third century.

Supreme Court   12.95

DISCARDED BY
WEST HEMPSTEAD
PUBLIC LIBRARY

West Hempstead Public Library
West Hempstead, N. Y.

WH F

The judicial Power of the United States, shall be vested in one supreme Court, and in such inferior Courts as the Congress may from time to time ordain and establish.
—Constitution of the United States
Article III, Section 1

INTO THE THIRD CENTURY

THE
SUPREME
COURT

By

RICHARD B. BERNSTEIN

and

JEROME AGEL

WALKER AND COMPANY
NEW YORK

Copyright © 1989 by Jerome Agel and Richard B. Bernstein

All rights reserved. No part of this book may be
reproduced or transmitted in any form or by any means,
electronic or mechanical, including photocopying,
recording, or by any information storage and retrieval
system, without permission in writing from the Publisher.

First published in the United States of America in 1989
by the Walker Publishing Company, Inc.

Published simultaneously in Canada by Thomas Allen & Son
Canada, Limited, Markham, Ontario.

Library of Congress Cataloging-in-Publication Data

Bernstein, Richard B., 1956–
    Into the third century. The supreme court / by Richard B.
    Bernstein and Jerome Agel.
        p.   cm.
    Includes index.
    Summary: A history of the Supreme Court which explores
    such ideas as judicial review and federalism, introduces
    Justices who have shaped our history and our law, and assesses
    the modern Court.
    ISBN 0-8027-6834-2.   ISBN 0-8027-6835-0 (lib. bdg.)
    1. United States. Supreme Court—History—Juvenile
literature.
2. Judicial power—United States—History—Juvenile
literature.
[1. United States. Supreme Court—History.]   I. Agel, Jerome.
II. Title.
KF8742.Z9B47 1989
347.73'26'09—dc19
[347.3073509]   88-21027
                                                            CIP
                                                             AC

Printed in the United States of America

10 9 8 7 6 5 4 3 2 1

Into the Third Century

For my mother, my first teacher, with love.

R. B. B.

The Supreme Court

For Christa Tillman-Young, Adam Tillman-Young, Noah Tillman-Young, and Luke Tillman-Young . . . future leaders of the rising generation.

R. B. B.

CONTENTS

INTRODUCTION

The people of the United States govern themselves under a Constitution now two centuries old. It was written in the days of horse-drawn carriages and sailing ships, of powdered wigs and knee-breeches. Its authors, a few dozen men from twelve struggling states along the Atlantic Ocean, had never heard of personal computers or space satellites or nuclear reactors, of airplanes or railroads or automobiles.

The Constitution does not govern this country. "We the People of the United States" do that. We choose the people who will make our laws, enforce them, and settle disputes arising under them. Our Constitution establishes three branches of government: the legislative, the executive, and the judiciary. Each of these three branches has the power to check or restrain the other two branches. The three branches have often worked together and, just as often, they have worked against one another. They are held in a delicate balance by the commands of the Constitution. This system of government has turned out to be strong enough to deal with national problems, flexible enough to adapt to changing times and conditions, and limited enough to avoid damaging our rights.

This is one of three books about the central institutions of our system of government: Congress, the Presidency, and the Supreme Court. Reading all three volumes will introduce you to two centuries of American history, as well as to the history of each institution. You will also learn about the leading figures in each institution's history—the people who have helped to make our system of government work. Some important events appear in only one or two of the three books. This is because our system of government divides power among the three branches of our government. Therefore, some major problems in our history have been the business of only one branch or of two of the three.

CHAPTER ONE

THE BIRTH OF THE SUPREME COURT

Throughout our history, the value at the heart of our political system has been "Liberty under Law." In 1776, the Revolutionary pamphleteer Thomas Paine boasted: "In America the law is king." The Constitution of the United States, written eleven years later, is a special kind of law—a *fundamental* law. It is different from, more important than, ordinary laws. Article VI of the Constitution says, "This Constitution . . . shall be the supreme law of the land."

Chief Justice John Marshall declared in 1803, "It is emphatically the province and duty of the judiciary department to say what the law is." Article III of the Constitution assigns this power, the judicial power, to the United States Supreme Court and to whatever lower federal courts Congress sets up. How the federal courts have shaped American history—and have been shaped by that history—is the subject of this book.

The first charter of government for the United States, the Articles of Confederation, did not provide for a federal court system. (The Articles were proposed in 1777, a year after the Declaration of Independence, and adopted by all thirteen states by March 1781.) The Confederation Congress appointed committees of its members to work out boundary and other disputes between states. A special body, the Court of Appeals in Cases of Capture, was created to hear cases having to do with piracy, shipping, and maritime law.

One reason that many Americans came to believe in the 1780s that the Articles needed to be revised or replaced was that there was no impartial system of courts where citizens of different states or subjects of foreign countries could get fair decisions in their lawsuits.

When they wrote the Constitution in Philadelphia in 1787, the delegates to the Federal Convention did not spend much time on the federal judiciary. They agreed to provide for a Supreme Court, but they did not say how many members the Court should have. They left it to Congress to decide this question and to decide whether there would be any federal courts below the Supreme Court and how these courts would fit together. The delegates also decided that the President would appoint all federal judges, but that the Senate would have to *confirm* these appointments. These judges would serve for life unless removed from office for serious misdeeds. The delegates also defined the "judicial power" of the United States. They figured that if the Constitution were adopted, the first Congress would fill the gaps. This is exactly what happened.

On September 24, 1789, President George Washington signed into law the bill we now call the Judiciary Act of 1789. This is the most important federal statute ever adopted under the Constitution. It established the structure and authority of the federal courts that would interpret the U.S. Constitution and federal law. Although the Judiciary Act of 1789 has been amended many times since it was enacted, it is still law.

Think of the federal court system as a pyramid. In keeping with the Constitution, the original Judiciary Act put the Supreme Court at the top of the pyramid. (It is still there today.) Under the 1789 law, the next level was the *federal circuit courts,* and the third, or bottom, level was the *federal district courts.* The federal court system exists side by side with the state court systems. Each state has its own system of trial courts and appeals courts. Although many issues of law are ultimately settled by the federal courts—and, specifically, the U.S. Supreme Court—many issues of law that don't raise problems under the Constitution or federal law are handled by the state courts. This complex system of federal courts and state courts protects the constitutional value of *federalism*— the division of authority between the federal government and state and local governments.

Both the federal circuit courts and the federal district courts were *trial courts.* People could sue each other in circuit court or in district court. However, the district courts were authorized to hear only a few limited types of cases under the customs laws passed by Congress. The main trial courts in the federal system were the circuit courts.

The Judiciary Act of 1789 divided the United States into three *circuits:* the Eastern (New York, Massachusetts, Connecticut, New Hampshire, and Maine [then still part of Massachusetts]); the Middle (New Jersey, Pennsylvania, Maryland, Delaware, Virginia, and Kentucky [then part of Virginia]); and the Southern (South Carolina and Georgia). North Carolina and Rhode Island had not yet ratified the Constitution by September 1789 and therefore could not be included within the judicial system.

Each state had its own federal district court and judge. Kentucky and Maine also had their own district courts and judges, even though they were not yet states. They were *territories,* waiting for Congress to decide that they were ready to become states.

The three circuit courts consisted of two Supreme Court Justices and the district judge for each state or territory where the circuit court would meet. The Justices had to travel around each circuit—"ride" the circuit, by horse or stage-coach—twice a year. One Justice assigned to the Southern Circuit calculated that he had to travel nearly 2,000 miles on each trip. When North Carolina (in 1789) and Rhode Island (in 1790) ratified the Constitution, Congress amended the Judiciary Act to create district courts for each state and to add them to the Southern and Eastern Circuits, respectively. Congress continued to restructure the federal courts as more states joined the Union.

The Judiciary Act created a six-member Supreme Court, with a Chief Justice and five Associate Justices. They set the number of Justices at six to provide two Justices for each of the three circuits. Later, as more states joined the Union, Congress added Justices to the Supreme Court.

The Supreme Court was given the authority to hear and decide appeals from lower federal courts and to hear and decide appeals from decisions of state courts on matters affecting the Constitution or federal laws. Because the government created by the Constitution was so new, the Justices had to wait several years for their first case.

President Washington named the first Justices of the Supreme Court, and the Senate quickly approved his choices. John Jay of New York was the first Chief Justice. He was forty-four years old, a veteran of state and national politics and foreign diplomacy. He had been the Confederation's Secretary for Foreign Affairs, the author of the New York constitution of 1777, and New York's first chief justice under that constitution. In 1787–1788, he had also helped to lead the battle in New York to adopt the Constitution. As part of that battle, he had written five of the famous *Federalist* essays explaining and defending the Constitution.

James Wilson of Pennsylvania had wanted to be Chief Justice but had to be content with an appointment as an Associate Justice. He was one of the greatest lawyers in America—some said that his mind was a blaze of light—and

COLLECTION OF THE SUPREME COURT OF THE UNITED STATES

John Jay, the first Chief Justice (1789–1795), was an able judge but disliked circuit riding, because it was an excessive burden on the Supreme Court. Six years after tendering his resignation to President George Washington, Jay refused to become Chief Justice again, even though the Senate had confirmed his reappointment by President John Adams.

a principal member of the Federal Convention. Two other veterans of the Convention were also named to the Court: John Rutledge of South Carolina and John Blair of Virginia. Washington also nominated William Cushing, a notable Massachusetts lawyer and judge who was a leading supporter of the Constitution, and Robert Hanson Harrison of Maryland, a respected judge and a comrade-in-arms from the Revolution. But Harrison had just been named to Maryland's highest judicial post and was in poor health. So he declined the appointment to the Supreme Court, even though the Senate had already confirmed him. (As it turned out, he died the week before the Supreme Court was to begin its first session.) By this time, North Carolina had ratified the Constitution, so President Washington nominated James Iredell, the leader of that state's pro-Constitution forces, to the seat refused by Harrison, and the Senate confirmed him.

The Supreme Court convened for the first time on February 4, 1790, in New York City, the first capital of the United States. This first session was one of ceremony rather than serious business. The Court began to hear and decide cases only after it moved with the rest of the federal government to the new capital at Philadelphia at the end of 1790.

In 1793, President Washington wanted advice about measures he planned to take to keep the United States from being drawn into the war between Great Britain and France. He asked his Secretary of State, Thomas Jefferson, to send a letter to the Justices asking whether his plans were constitutional. To Washington's and Jefferson's surprise, the Justices refused this request for advice. They reminded the President that the Constitution authorized them only to hear actual cases and controversies. Under the Constitution, the phrase "cases and controversies" means disputes where actual rights, injuries, or claims of authority are at stake and the parties to the case or controversy have something to gain or lose. The Justices reminded the President that they could not use their power as Justices of the Supreme Court to answer questions before there was a real dispute for them to decide. This decision *not* to act was extremely important. It confirmed that the courts were independent from the other parts of the government.

The circuit courts were the most active part of the new court system in its first decade. As the Justices traveled throughout the country, they confirmed to the people that the government created by the Constitution was real and powerful.

Each session of the circuit courts opened with pomp and

pageantry. The judges (the Supreme Court Justices riding that circuit and the local federal district judge) convened federal *grand juries*—bodies of citizens who were to inquire whether the laws of the United States had been violated and who should be tried in court for violating those laws. The presiding Justice would deliver a speech to the members of the grand jury instructing them about their duty and explaining to them and the people generally the principles of the Constitution.

One of the first cases to reach the Supreme Court caused a major controversy. Chisholm, a citizen of South Carolina, was the executor of an estate. (An *executor* is the person having legal responsibility for the possessions, or *estate*, of a dead person.) He discovered that the state of Georgia still owed his late friend money for war supplies that the dead man had sold to the state during the Revolution. To recover this money for his friend's estate, Chisholm sued the state of Georgia in federal court.

In 1787–1788, during the ratification controversy, the Constitution's supporters had assured the people that the Constitution would not allow federal courts to hear a suit by a citizen of one state against another state. But the Supreme Court surprised the nation—the Justices upheld Chisholm's claim.

Chisholm v. Georgia caused a huge public outcry. The states feared that they would be buried in lawsuits. During the Revolution, the new state governments had forced people who were still loyal to Great Britain and King George III— the Loyalists—to give up their land and their money and flee the country. The states treated them this way because the Loyalists had refused to swear to support the Revolution. Now, the state governments worried, the *Chisholm* case would be a green light for the Loyalists to sue to get their land and their money back. Congress therefore proposed a constitutional amendment to strip the federal courts of the power to hear suits against a state by citizens of another state or of foreign countries. The states quickly ratified the proposal, and in 1798 it became the Eleventh Amendment. It was the first amendment to be added to the Constitution since the adoption of the Bill of Rights, the first ten amendments, in 1791. The Eleventh Amendment is the only constitutional amendment limiting the powers of the federal courts, and it was the first amendment to overturn a decision of the Supreme Court.

Chief Justice John Jay was an able and respected judge, but he did not like having to travel throughout several states twice each year. In 1792, he let his friends put his name forward as a candidate for Governor of New York. If Jay had won, he would have resigned from the Court to become Governor. Although Jay did not campaign, he lost the election only because his opponents "fixed" the counting of the votes.

In 1794, George Washington wanted to ease American relations with Great Britain. He asked Chief Justice Jay to go to Great Britain to negotiate a commercial treaty. Jay was abroad for more than a year. He returned from London in 1795 with a treaty that pleased Americans who liked Great Britain but outraged those who distrusted their old enemy. On his arrival in New York City, the Chief Justice discovered to his surprise and delight that he had been put forward again as a candidate for Governor of New York, and that this time the voters had elected him. Jay immediately resigned from the Court.

The President chose former Associate Justice John Rutledge to succeed Jay as Chief Justice. "Dictator John" was a powerful South Carolina politician who had resigned from the Court in 1791. He had never served with his fellow Justices in sessions of the Supreme Court, although he had carried out his duty to "ride circuit" in the South. The Senate was not in session when Chief Justice Jay resigned, so Washington made a *recess appointment*. This device, authorized by the

Constitution, meant that Rutledge could hold the job of Chief Justice until the Senate met to vote on confirmation.

Rutledge's nomination ran into trouble almost immediately because of speeches he had made attacking the Jay Treaty. President Washington was astonished and annoyed but did not withdraw Rutledge's nomination. Also, rumors spread that the nominee was losing his mind. The Senate rejected Rutledge. Scandalmongers whispered that "Dictator John" tried to kill himself when he heard that the Senate had turned him down. Rutledge indeed went mad in the last five years of his life. He was a shattered wreck when he died in 1800.

Washington tried again—this time with Oliver Ellsworth of Connecticut, another veteran of the Federal Convention and one of the three Senators who had drafted the Judiciary Act of 1789. Ellsworth won quick confirmation by the Senate. The Senators decided to ignore his odd habits of taking snuff constantly and talking to himself.

Under Ellsworth, the Supreme Court decided another major case, known as the "Carriage Tax Case." Congress had passed a law at the suggestion of Secretary of the Treasury Alexander Hamilton imposing a tax on carriages—which in the 1790s were what limousines are today, a means of travel available only to the rich. Some Americans refused to pay the tax, charging that it was unconstitutional because it violated the Constitution's ban on "direct" taxes (Article I, Section 9). But no one knew what the Constitution's ban on direct taxes meant; in 1787, delegate Rufus King of Massachusetts had raised the question in the Federal Convention, but nobody could give him an answer.

At the invitation of Attorney General William Bradford, Hamilton came out of retirement to defend the constitutionality of the carriage tax before the Supreme Court. Hamilton's formal presentation—what lawyers call *arguing the case*—was a great success with the Justices, and with the fashionable people of Philadelphia who had come to hear him. The Justices upheld the tax. This was the first time that the Supreme Court had exercised the power of *judicial review*— the power to say whether a statute properly adopted by the United States or a state is nonetheless invalid because it violates the Constitution.

For several reasons, the Court declined in popularity and prestige in the late 1790s. The Rutledge controversy had not helped. The Eleventh Amendment, overruling *Chisholm v. Georgia*, had not helped, either. Also, Justice James Wilson died in 1798, bankrupt and broken in mind and spirit, in an inn in Edenton, North Carolina. Wilson had been a friend and adviser of the richest man in the United States, Robert Morris, a fellow Pennsylvanian, who had been at the Federal Convention and in the 1790s was a Senator. Morris was a daring speculator in land, stocks, and bonds, and Wilson followed Morris's advice with his own investments. When Morris's financial empire collapsed, Wilson fell with him. The Justice's creditors hounded him from place to place with demands for repayment and threats of lawsuits and debtors' prison—a special jail where those who could not pay their debts were held behind bars until they could pay. Wilson's fate seriously damaged the reputation of the Supreme Court.

Finally, the Supreme Court was being drawn into politics as political parties developed and the Federalists and Republicans (*not* the same Republican party we have today) fought bitterly with each other. In 1798, during an undeclared naval war with France, the Federalist-dominated Congress passed the Alien and Sedition Acts. The Alien Act made it hard for people from foreign countries to become American citizens, and it gave the government sweeping power to throw them out of the country. The Sedition Act punished anyone who said or published anything that might injure the reputation of the President or other government officials. Under the Sedition Act, Federalists prosecuted many Republicans, including editors and printers, for their writings against government policy, even though Thomas Jefferson, James Madison, and their supporters argued that the law was unconstitutional. The Republicans grew to distrust and fear Federalist judges like Supreme Court Justice Samuel Chase of Maryland, and planned to revenge themselves someday.

In 1800, President John Adams dramatically turned government policy upside-down. He cleared out his Cabinet and appointed Chief Justice Ellsworth to make peace with France. While in Europe, Ellsworth resigned this appointment and the Chief Justiceship because of poor health. Adams offered the post to Governor John Jay, and the Senate confirmed the nomination, but Jay turned the President down. He would not go back to the federal courts as long as the exhausting system of circuit riding was in force. Adams then turned to his new Secretary of State, John Marshall of Virginia, and the Senate confirmed Marshall without protest.

CHAPTER TWO

JOHN MARSHALL

John Marshall was born in Virginia in 1755. He was a veteran of the Revolutionary War who had been with George Washington at Valley Forge. His entire legal education was six months of law lectures at the College of William and Mary in Virginia. (Law schools—the way lawyers are trained today—were not developed until the nineteenth century.) Marshall was a leading supporter of the Constitution in the Virginia ratifying convention of June 1788. He was also a national hero, having been one of the three American diplomats who refused French attempts of bribery during a failed diplomatic mission that was a major cause of the undeclared war between the United States and France (1798–1800). Marshall's popular role in the "XYZ Affair" won him election to the House of Representatives. He served there until Adams named him Secretary of State in 1800.

Marshall was the most important of a series of appointments made by John Adams in the last days of his Presidency. Adams and the Federalists had been defeated at the polls by Thomas Jefferson and the Republicans in 1800. But, as they endured the swamps and muddy roads of the new capital city

COLLECTION OF THE SUPREME COURT OF THE UNITED STATES

John Marshall, the fourth and the greatest Chief Justice (1801–1835), did more than anyone else to make the Supreme Court a respected and powerful branch of the national government. His judicial opinions are foundations of American constitutional law.

of Washington, D.C., they were determined to hold on to at least one branch of government. In a *lame-duck session* between the elections and the end of their terms of office, the Federalist-dominated Congress passed the Judiciary Act of 1801. It reformed the 1789 statute and created many new judgeships for Federalists. Adams then nominated judges and the Senate confirmed them, and Adams stayed up until long after midnight on March 3, 1801, his last full day in office, signing the commissions for these "midnight judges."

In the weeks before President Thomas Jefferson's new Republican Administration took office, John Marshall was Secretary of State and Chief Justice at the same time. He was so busy that he forgot to deliver *commissions*, a formal certificate declaring the person named in it to have been appointed to a federal office, to some of the "midnight judges," one of his duties as Secretary of State. James Madison, Jefferson's new Secretary of State, found the undelivered commissions in Marshall's former desk, and he and Jefferson decided not to deliver them. Because the commissions had not been delivered, the uncommissioned judges could not take office.

President Adams had appointed William Marbury to be a justice of the peace for the District of Columbia. All the paperwork had been completed, but Marbury had not received his commission. Marbury wanted his job and chose to "go to court" to get it—a decision that caused John Marshall, James Madison, and Thomas Jefferson all kinds of embarrassment and confusion. It became one of the most important milestones in the history of the Constitution, the Supreme Court, and the United States.

Marbury went straight to the top: He filed a lawsuit in the U.S. Supreme Court asking for a special legal document called a *writ of mandamus*—a document requiring a government official to do his job. This writ, addressed to Secretary of State Madison, demanded that Madison turn over Marbury's commission.

Chief Justice Marshall was caught in an impossible dilemma—or so Jefferson and Madison thought. In the first place, Marshall's own failure to deliver the commissions had caused this mess. (In the early days of the federal courts, there were few formal rules requiring judges to disqualify themselves in cases in which they were personally involved.) If Marshall granted Marbury's request for a writ of mandamus, Jefferson and Madison could ignore the writ because the Court seemed so weak and lacking in authority. If he denied Marbury's request, it would look like an admission that the Court had no power. Either way, the Court would look ridiculous. The dilemma became even more troubling when the Republican-dominated Congress passed the Judiciary Act of 1802, repealing the 1801 Act (getting rid of the "midnight judge-ships") and suspending the Supreme Court's sessions for 1802. The 1802 Act made it clear that Congress could strangle the federal courts if it wanted to.

On February 24, 1803, John Marshall delivered his opinion for a unanimous Supreme Court in the case of *Marbury v. Madison*. He asked three questions. First, did Marbury have a right to seek help from the federal courts, as Marbury claimed? Yes, the Chief Justice declared, and he took the opportunity to read a stinging lecture to the Jefferson Administration about its duty to obey the law—a duty it had ignored by refusing to deliver Marbury's commission. Second, Marshall asked whether a writ of mandamus was the right remedy for the injury that the Jefferson Administration had caused Mar-bury. Of course it was. After all, Chief Justice Marshall explained, there are two kinds of things that government officials do:

• First, government officials think about policy and make decisions. The courts cannot control such exercises of discre-tion.

• Second, government officials do the ordinary, "mechan-ical" acts that are part of their job, such as delivering judicial commissions.

A writ of mandamus is the right remedy for a government official's refusal to do "mechanical" acts that the law requires.

The third question was trickiest: Was the cure for Marbury's problem a writ of mandamus issued by the Supreme Court? Marshall explained that the Court had very limited powers under the Constitution to hear cases brought straight to it, as Marbury had done. The Constitution's term for the class of cases that may be begun in the Supreme Court is *original jurisdiction*. The Constitution, Marshall noted, does not list writs of mandamus as part of the Court's original jurisdiction.

But one section of the Judiciary Act of 1789 *did* list writs of mandamus as part of that original jurisdiction. Which should the Court follow: the Constitution or a statute?

According to Marshall, the Constitution is a *fundamental law* that is above ordinary laws. If the Constitution does not authorize the Court to grant a writ of mandamus in its original jurisdiction and the statute does, something must be wrong with the statute. The statute is *unconstitutional* and must be null and void. Therefore, the section of the Judiciary Act of 1789 permitting Marbury to go straight to the Supreme Court for a writ of mandamus was unconstitutional. The Court could not grant Marbury the help that he sought.

Marshall surprised everyone. The Chief Justice had declared that the Court had no power to help Marbury. But he also had shown that the Court had a huge and important power to declare acts of Congress unconstitutional. (Most people had forgotten about the "Carriage Tax Case," or did not realize that the power to uphold a law as constitutional suggested an equal power to throw out a law as unconstitutional.) The Court was the final authority on what the Constitution meant—unless, as in the case of *Chisholm v. Georgia* and the subsequent Eleventh Amendment, the people amended the Constitution to overturn a decision of the Supreme Court.

President Jefferson was furious. He believed that Marshall had declared war on his Administration and would use the power of judicial review as his weapon in that war. But Marshall had done a brilliant job with *Marbury v. Madison*. He had actually denied that the Court had the power to do anything specific about the Jefferson Administration's misconduct in the matter of the "missing commissions." Marshall also had avoided a battle over the repeal of the Judiciary Act of 1801, the law that had created the "midnight judgeships." He clearly understood that those who live and run away will live to fight another day. But Marshall had asserted that the

Supreme Court had the authority and the responsibility to control the actions of the other branches of the federal government by interpreting the Constitution.

Jefferson and his allies believed that each branch of the federal government had an equal power and responsibility to interpret the Constitution. They rejected Marshall's argument that the Court should have the last word unless overruled by the people through a constitutional amendment. The President and the Republican-dominated Congress decided that it was necessary to clip the Court's wings.

The Constitution provides that all federal officials, including the President and federal judges, can be impeached (formally accused) by the House of Representatives and tried by the Senate for "treason, bribery, or other High Crimes and misdemeanors." Impeachment is the Constitution's method for removing federal officials who are corrupt or who abuse their powers.

President Jefferson and the Republican-controlled Congress determined to use the impeachment power to rein in the federal courts. Their first target was a New Hampshire Federalist named John Pickering. Pickering, the federal district judge for New Hampshire, was old, sick, and a drunkard. He had not committed any "impeachable offense," but that did not matter to Congress. The House impeached him and the Senate removed him from office. (Pickering probably had no idea what had happened to him.) The supporters of the impeachment campaign argued that impeachment was just "the enquiry, by the two Houses of Congress, whether the office of any public man might not be better filled by another."

Congress then went after a Supreme Court Justice: old, fat Samuel Chase of Maryland. He had denounced Republicans from the bench during trials under the Sedition Act in his circuit court. The House impeached Chase on the same theory the members had used to oust Judge Pickering. Everyone knew that if Chase was convicted, Chief Justice John Marshall would be the next target.

Chase's trial in the Senate produced an unexpected obstacle to his conviction: Vice President Aaron Burr. Burr had shot and killed Alexander Hamilton in a duel in July 1804 and had been indicted for murder by grand juries in New Jersey and New York. Although Burr was never tried on these charges, his career was almost at an end. In fact, the Republicans had already picked New York's Governor George Clinton to replace Burr as the party's nominee for Vice President in 1804. But Burr had a few months to go in his term as Vice President. The Constitution required that he preside over the trial of Justice Chase, and Burr carried out the task with dignity and fairness, winning the respect even of his political enemies. Chase was acquitted, and the Jefferson Administration's war with the judiciary was at an end.

For the next thirty years, John Marshall presided over the Supreme Court. He delighted John Adams, who said that the Marshall appointment was the best legacy of his Presidency. Marshall still infuriated Thomas Jefferson. Jefferson repeatedly denounced the "twistifications" of the "crafty chief judge" in letters to his friends, but Marshall prevailed.

As the leader and the spokesman of the Supreme Court, Chief Justice Marshall established many principles at the core of our constitutional law. He ruled that the Constitution authorized the Supreme Court to declare state laws unconstitutional and that the states had to obey the decisions of the Supreme Court. He held that a person who lost a case in the highest court of a state could appeal that decision to the United States Supreme Court if the case posed a question of federal constitutional law. He declared that the federal government was the creature of the people of the United States, not the tool of the state governments. It was the supreme authority in the federal system of government, second only to the people themselves.

Many of the Marshall Court's decisions had to do with the *commerce clause* of the Constitution. Article I, Section 8 gives Congress the power to regulate commerce among the states. What does this power mean? How far does it reach? When can states pass laws regulating business? When must the states' power bow to that of Congress? Are there areas where the states may not act, even though Congress has not acted? John Marshall's Supreme Court handed down major decisions on all these questions.

The commerce clause may not seem controversial to us, but in the early years of the United States it was a source of great political and constitutional dispute. Many Americans did not trust strong central government; they preferred to have government stay as close to the people as possible. They preferred government to be local and small scale. But Chief Justice Marshall saw that many problems affecting trade and commerce were national problems, not local ones. He remembered that one reason for the movement to write and adopt the Constitution was to give the nation's government the power to establish uniform rules for interstate commerce. He understood that asking for local solutions to national problems would only make the problems worse because there would be too many schemes to solve them, all conflicting with one another and making it nearly impossible for trade to take place across state lines. John Marshall was faithful to this nationalist vision.

Marshall had support on the Court from young Joseph Story. Story was a Massachusetts lawyer and politician who was only thirty-two years old when President James Madison named him to the Supreme Court to succeed William Cushing, who had died in 1810. Story was brilliant and energetic. He wrote many fat commentaries on American law and, as the first law professor at Harvard University, helped to found the nation's oldest law school. He still found time to sit as a Supreme Court Justice and to ride circuit in the New England states. Story was just as enthusiastic for national power and a strong Constitution as was John Marshall. Story looked up to Marshall as if Marshall were his father, and Marshall considered Story almost to be his son. The two men worked side by side for more than twenty years, from 1812 to Marshall's death in 1835.

John Marshall held the office of Chief Justice for thirty-four years, longer than any other man. His tenure spanned the terms of six Presidents. When he died, legend has it that the Liberty Bell hanging in Philadelphia's Independence Hall tolled so loudly and stubbornly in his honor that it cracked. Another great Supreme Court Justice, Oliver Wendell Holmes, Jr., declared in 1901 (the centennial of Marshall's appointment to the Supreme Court) that if one person were chosen to represent American law, that person would be John Marshall.

Holmes thought that Marshall's greatness was partly an accident: "Part of greatness consists in being *there*" (that is, being in the right place at the right time). But Marshall had many talents. He was willing to shoulder the work involved in writing *opinions*, the formal statements of the reasoning of the Court in deciding a case. In writing those opinions, he had a remarkable ability to make a difficult and complex legal argument seem simple and clear. He was also charming, winning over even stubborn men like Justice William Johnson. President Jefferson had appointed Johnson to combat Marshall, but Johnson found the Chief Justice extremely persuasive. Even on those rare occasions when Johnson disagreed with the Chief Justice, he nearly always chose to sit silently as the Chief Justice read the "opinion of the Court" rather than to express his disagreement in a dissenting opinion.

Today, we are used to the idea that when the Supreme Court decides a case, one Justice will write the *opinion of the Court* and any Justice who is outvoted can write a *dissenting opinion* (explaining why he or she disagrees and setting out arguments for this position). But John Marshall invented the opinion of the Court. Previously, as the judges did in England, each Supreme Court Justice had delivered his opinion on the case before the Court. You could figure out the result by counting up the votes, but you did not have a single clear statement of what the majority of the Justices thought. Marshall's willingness to write opinions for the Court, his skills in writing them so as to command the support of his colleagues, and his practice never to dissent from a Court decision he disagreed with made the opinion of the Court a central feature of the workings of the Supreme Court.

In all these ways—in the substance of the cases that the Court decided under his leadership and in his shaping of the Court's place in the constitutional system and its methods of doing business—John Marshall laid the foundation for the Supreme Court as we know it today.

CHAPTER THREE

ROGER B. TANEY

To succeed John Marshall as Chief Justice, President Andrew Jackson appointed his Attorney General, Roger B. Taney (pronounced *tawny*) of Maryland. Many conservatives, including Marshall's friend Justice Joseph Story, were appalled. Taney was a Roman Catholic—and many Americans feared the power of the Catholic Church. Taney had backed Jackson's efforts to crush the Second Bank of the United States. He was also a critic of John Marshall and the Supreme Court. Senator Daniel Webster of Massachusetts, one of the strongest supporters of the Marshall Court, wrote in a private letter, "Judge Story thinks the Supreme Court is *gone,* and I think so too."

Like all other Presidents, Jackson wanted a Supreme Court that would hand down decisions to his liking. He had been suspicious of the Marshall Court and once had refused to enforce one of Chief Justice Marshall's rulings defending the rights of the Cherokee Indians against the greed of the state of Georgia. With a man he could trust in the Chief Justice's chair, Jackson believed that he could rest easier. Besides,

Taney was one of the ablest lawyers of his day, a worthy successor to Chief Justice Marshall.

Taney served as Chief Justice for twenty-nine years—a record second only to Marshall's. His tenure spanned the terms of ten Presidents. The Taney Court refined and developed the expansive ideas of federal power and judicial power symbolic of John Marshall. Despite Justice Story's despairing charges in his dissenting opinions, it is likely that Marshall generally would have approved of the work of the Taney Court. One of its most important achievements was to strike a balance between the federal power to regulate interstate commerce and the states' *police powers,* that is, the state governments' power to make laws or take other actions to protect the health, safety, welfare, and morals of their citizens.

If such achievements were the only important legacies of the Taney Court, Roger B. Taney would be generally remembered as one of the greatest of our Justices. But we remember the Taney Court today for the *Dred Scott* case, the single greatest blunder ever committed by a federal court and a terrible stain on American history.

Dred Scott was a slave, born in the slave state of Missouri. His owner had taken him briefly from Missouri into the free state of Illinois, where slavery was illegal by state law and under the terms of the congressional Missouri Compromise of 1820 (by which Congress declared that new states north of a line drawn across the Louisiana Purchase would be free states and new states south of that line would be slave states), and then back to Missouri. Antislavery lawyers and politicians filed a lawsuit on Scott's behalf against John F. A. Sanford, his legal owner. They sought Scott's freedom on the ground that he had become free when his previous owner had taken him into a free state.

The *Dred Scott* case moved quietly through the federal court system. When it reached the Supreme Court, the trouble started. The majority of the Court at first agreed that because Scott was from Missouri, his status should be determined by that state's law. Justice Samuel Nelson began drafting the Court's opinion to state that narrow holding. But Chief Justice Taney and other proslavery Justices egged on antislavery Justice John McLean. McLean was a cantankerous troublemaker who had talked often about running for President. He took the bait and announced to his colleagues that he would write a broad dissent from the case attacking the institution of slavery. To the irritation of Justice Nelson, Chief Justice Taney took the opportunity to write an opinion answering McLean.

Taney had reasons of his own to write a broad opinion analyzing the constitutional issues posed by slavery. He did not personally like slavery—indeed, he had freed his own slaves some years before—but he believed that slavery was protected by the Constitution. The Chief Justice frowned on the many attempts by Senators and Representatives to work out compromises between North and South to control the spread of slavery into the new states and territories of the United States. The *Dred Scott* case seemed to be the perfect occasion for the Court to resolve the national controversy over slavery and the Constitution once and for all.

In the 1850s, four general positions existed on the slavery issue. The Supreme Court had to choose one of them to decide the *Dred Scott* case:

- *The antislavery view:* Slavery at least should be contained to those states where it had already been established, but eventually it must be abolished throughout the United States. To the extent that the Constitution protected slavery and slaveholders' rights, it was evil—"a compromise with death," as several abolitionists (those who wanted to do away with slavery) called it.
- *The old moderate view:* The issue of slavery could and

should be compromised in Congress by Senators and Representatives from the North, South, and West. Congressional "peace treaties" such as the Missouri Compromise of 1820 and the Compromise of 1850 would limit the spread of slavery but not choke it off. This view was developed by an earlier generation of politicians, led by Henry Clay of Kentucky.

• *The new moderate view:* Slavery could be adopted or rejected by the voters of a territory organizing to become a state but otherwise should stay as it was. This view's leading advocate was Senator Stephen A. Douglas (Democrat–Illinois), who called it "popular sovereignty."

• *The proslavery view:* Slavery was a positive good for slaveowners and slaves alike. Slaves were property protected by the Constitution's safeguards of private property. Any attempt to abolish slavery, to limit it, or to keep it out of any part of the Union was a violation of the Constitution.

The *Dred Scott* decision came as a bombshell to the country when the Court announced it on March 6, 1857. But Taney and some of the other Justices on both sides of the case had "leaked" the decision to several politicians, including the new President, James Buchanan of Pennsylvania. In his Inaugural Address two days before the Court's announcement, Buchanan predicted that the Court would soon produce a definitive, final answer to the slavery controversy, and he urged all Americans to obey it. Buchanan and those who thought as he did believed that the Court's decision would dispose of slavery as a political issue. They were dead wrong.

The Court ruled, seven to two, against Dred Scott's bid for freedom. Although Taney's opinion did not command an absolute majority of the Justices, it drew the most attention because Taney was the Chief Justice. By contrast, Justice Nelson stuck to his narrowly drawn opinion ruling against Scott on the basis of Missouri law. A few Justices sided with Nelson, but his opinion was generally ignored.

Taney declared that the Constitution clearly protected slavery. Any attempts to limit or choke off slavery's expansion violated the document. Even the old Missouri Compromise of 1820 was unconstitutional. Taney's opinion also killed off the "popular sovereignty" theory of slavery in the territories. He even declared that black persons were not—and could not be—citizens, and they had no rights that white Americans were bound to respect.

In short, Taney ruled that slavery was valid everywhere and could be taken anywhere in the United States. He even implied that slaveholders could take their slaves into a free state and hold them there as slaves, even though the state's laws prohibited slavery. His opinion read the Constitution as a proslavery charter of government, confirming the worst fears of the abolitionists and frustrating moderate attempts to compromise the issue.

Taney's opinion in *Dred Scott* infuriated opponents of slavery, and they flocked to join the newly organized Republican Party (a party claiming descent from that of Thomas Jefferson). The Republicans maintained that the decision did not settle the slavery issue once and for all. They stepped up their campaign against slavery and promised to work to overturn the *Dred Scott* decision by legitimate means. Many moderates, disappointed by what they saw as a proslavery power grab, also joined the Republicans.

Dred Scott and John Sanford were virtually ignored in the controversy. Scott was freed despite the Court's decision, and he became a porter in a St. Louis hotel, where curious tourists and visitors came to see him. He died of tuberculosis a year or so after the decision. John Sanford (whose name had been misspelled Sandford in the Supreme Court's report of the case) ended his days in an insane asylum—driven mad, some said, by his role in the lawsuit. (Sanford was a New York abolitionist who probably never met Scott—he was involved only as a means to a greater end.)

Taney had delivered a terrible blow to the prestige and authority of the Supreme Court, but he did not realize the damage he had done with his opinion in the *Dred Scott* case. He watched in horror and anger as Republican Abraham Lincoln of Illinois, who had denounced the *Dred Scott* decision as unconstitutional and vowed to find a way to overturn it, won the 1860 Presidential election. In one of the great ironies of American history, Chief Justice Taney had to administer the oath of office to President Lincoln, on March 4, 1861. The two men soon loathed each other.

As Lincoln led resistance to the Southern states' attempts to leave the Union in 1861, Taney issued decision after decision (from the U.S. Circuit Court in Maryland) declaring each and every one of Lincoln's war measures unconstitutional. The President ignored the decisions. To anyone who claimed that he was violating the Constitution, Lincoln explained that he was trying to *save* the Constitution as a whole in a time of great crisis; it was absurd to let the whole system fall apart to avoid the risk of violating one of its parts.

Chief Justice Taney was convinced that President Lincoln was trying to become a dictator. He expected daily to see federal soldiers storm into his courtroom to arrest him. He would have welcomed arrest—it would have transformed him into a martyr to the rule of law. But Lincoln's refusal to acknowledge Taney's decisions was far more painful to the old Chief Justice. He died, tired and bitter, in 1864, the fourth year of the Civil War. Perhaps the worst pill that Taney had to swallow was the knowledge that Lincoln would get to name the next Chief Justice of the United States.

CHAPTER FOUR

SAVING FACE AND SHIFTING GROUND

The Supreme Court was very quiet during the Civil War. The Justices recognized that times of war are not good periods for the rule of law. They did not challenge many of the Administration's sweeping measures to advance the Union cause, though some arguably violated the Constitution. One glaring example was the President's decision to suspend the writ of *habeas corpus.* This legal document is a court order available to any imprisoned person who has a valid reason to argue that his imprisonment is not justified by law. The President acted on his own, though Article I, Section 9 of the Constitution implies that the approval of Congress is needed to suspend the writ. Congress later endorsed the President's decision, but critics of the Administration still had their doubts.

Also, President Lincoln and Congress did not treat the Supreme Court well during the Civil War. They had decided to expand the Supreme Court to ten members—the largest it has ever been. They did this in part to add a new Justice to handle circuit-riding duties in California and Oregon but also to make certain that there would be enough votes on the Court to support Administration measures to carry on the war effort. When Chief Justice Taney died, Lincoln used the new vacancy as a way to get rid of a thorn in his side. Treasury Secretary Salmon P. Chase of Ohio was an ardent abolitionist. Time and time again, he had stirred up trouble in Lincoln's Cabinet, and he seemed likely to challenge the President for the 1864 Republican Presidential nomination. President Lincoln got Chase out of the way by naming him the new Chief Justice, and the Senate confirmed the appointment.

After Lincoln was assassinated in April 1865, a few days after the Union's victory in the Civil War, the Supreme Court handed down a major decision attacking the federal government's measures against Northern opposition to the war. Some Northern Democrats, called "copperheads" after the poisonous snake of that name, had gone beyond merely denouncing the war. One of them, Lambdin P. Milligan, had led a plot to overthrow the governments of Ohio, Illinois, and Indiana and to release Confederate prisoners of war. A military court arrested and tried Milligan and sentenced him to death. But Milligan was a civilian, not a soldier. He argued that military courts had no power over civilians, and he sued in the federal circuit court in Indianapolis, Indiana, for a writ of *habeas corpus* to challenge the authority under which he was being held in military prison.

When the case reached the Supreme Court, the Justices agreed with Milligan. Lincoln's former campaign manager, Justice David Davis, delivered the opinion of the Court. If civilian courts were still open—and they were when Milligan was arrested—no one, not even Congress, could authorize military courts to try civilians. The Court declared that it had the authority to decide whether military necessity justified violations of constitutional rights.

The issues raised in the *Milligan* case were related to issues in other cases that the Court never got a chance to decide. These cases dealt with Civil War measures taken by the federal government and with policies adopted by Congress, called *Reconstruction*, to administer the defeated Southern states. Congress passed laws preventing the Court from hearing these cases. Congress exercised this authority under Article III, Section 1 of the Constitution to define the federal courts' *subject-matter jurisdiction*—that is, the courts' power to hear various kinds of cases. Chief Justice Chase and his colleagues had to concede that Congress had constitutional power to cut off jurisdiction, even to prevent the Court from hearing a case that had been within its jurisdiction when the case began. Congress, dominated by Northern Republicans, was reminding the courts who was boss.

Congress also wanted to remind the President who was boss. Vice President Andrew Johnson had succeeded to the Presidency when Lincoln was murdered. The new President soon broke with Congress over the government's treatment of the defeated Southern states.

The dispute between the President and Congress over Reconstruction grew into an ugly constitutional crisis which dragged the Court into the middle of the mess. When Justice John Catron died in 1865, Congress abolished his seat and, for good measure, reduced the Court from ten Justices to seven. Justices then sitting would not lose their seats, but Johnson could not replace the next two to die or resign. (The Court actually shrank to eight Justices as a result of this statute and the death in 1867 of Justice James M. Wayne.)

In early 1868, the House of Representatives decided to impeach the President. Some Representatives believed that he had violated the Constitution by refusing to enforce Reconstruction statutes that Congress had passed over his veto. Other Representatives argued that an impeachable offense was whatever a majority of the House and two-thirds of the Senate said it was—thus reviving the understanding of impeachment advocated by President Jefferson's supporters more than sixty years before.

Under the Constitution, the Chief Justice of the United

States presides over the trial of a President on charges of impeachment to ensure that the presiding officer is fair. (If the Vice President were to preside over the trial of the President, as he does in other impeachment trials, he might be tempted to influence the trial so that he could become President.) Thus, Chief Justice Chase presided over President Johnson's trial by the Senate. Following the example of Vice President Aaron Burr's handling of the Senate's trial of Justice Samuel Chase in 1805 (the Chief Justice was not related to old Samuel Chase), Chief Justice Chase presided with fairness. He refused to allow the trial to become a partisan brawl. The Senate voted to convict, but the vote was one short of the two-thirds required by the Constitution. Johnson thus stayed in office for the last nine months of his term. Chief Justice Chase's conduct saved the Presidency and helped to restore some of the Supreme Court's lost prestige.

General Ulysses S. Grant was elected President in 1868 to succeed Johnson, who left Washington in a bitter mood, not even waiting for the inauguration. The eighteenth President, a Republican, was popular with Congress and the nation because he had led the Union's armies to victory in the Civil War. Congress was so pleased by Grant's election that they rewarded him by passing a law increasing the size of the Supreme Court to nine Justices. This law undid the one that Congress had passed during Andrew Johnson's Presidency to deny him a chance to name a member of the Court. (Grant nominated former Secretary of War Edwin Stanton to fill the new seat, and Congress confirmed him. A seat on the Supreme Court had been Stanton's lifelong ambition, but Stanton died before he could accept.)

The Civil War left a legacy that became part of the Constitution. In 1868, the Fourteenth Amendment was ratified by the states. This was one of three amendments that historians call the *Civil War Amendments*. The Thirteenth Amendment, ratified in 1865, had abolished slavery. The

Fifteenth Amendment, ratified in 1870, recognized the right of American males to vote regardless of their race. The Fourteenth Amendment was, in many ways, the most important because it reshaped the structure of government set up by the Constitution:

1. It put the federal government above the states once and for all. The prewar system of federalism was a source of great controversy because politicians such as John C. Calhoun of South Carolina had argued that the Constitution was a compact, or agreement, among the states and that the federal government was the agent of the states. The Fourteenth Amendment made explicit what the force of the Union Army had already accomplished: The Union was supreme and preeminent.

2. It declared that persons born in the United States or persons who had become citizens of the United States were citizens of the United States *first* (rather than of individual states) and that the rights of citizenship of the United States outranked citizenship of a given state.

3. It declared that state and local governments could not deprive persons of life, liberty, or property without "due process of law" and that state and local governments could not deny persons "the equal protection of the laws."

At least one purpose of the Fourteenth Amendment was to ensure that the Civil Rights Act of 1866, the first law passed by Congress to protect the rights of Americans (specifically the freed slaves) against racial discrimination, was constitutional. It appeared that the Amendment also applied the Bill of Rights to limit the power of state and local governments to violate the rights protected by the first ten amendments to the Constitution. The Amendment seemed to overturn the 1833 Supreme Court decision in *Barron v. Baltimore* in which Chief Justice John Marshall had ruled that the first ten amendments limited only the powers of the federal government. But in 1873, in a series of cases known as the *Slaughter-*

house Cases, the Court limited the reach of the Fourteenth Amendment.

The state legislature of Louisiana had adopted as a public health measure a law that required the butchers of New Orleans to use one, and only one, designated slaughterhouse in that city. Butchers in New Orleans denounced the law as setting up a monopoly. Their lawyers tried to persuade the Supreme Court that the law deprived the butchers of private property without due process of law in violation of the Fourteenth Amendment. In effect, they claimed, the Fourteenth Amendment prohibited government from infringing the broad rights of the individual, including the right to conduct business as he or she saw fit.

This was the first major case to interpret the Fourteenth Amendment. The Justices split, five to four. Speaking for the majority, Justice Samuel Miller read the Amendment narrowly. He concluded that the Amendment protected only certain narrow, technical rights having to do with citizenship of the United States. Thus, the states were not barred from violating federal constitutional rights listed in the Bill of Rights; those amendments still limited the federal government only. Justice Miller also declared that the Amendment was intended only to protect the rights of the freed slaves. It had no larger purpose. Thus, the Louisiana slaughterhouse law was constitutional.

Justice Stephen J. Field dissented. He argued that private economic rights were indeed part of the "liberty" protected by the Amendment, and that the slaughterhouse law clearly violated that liberty. Field was joined by three other Justices.

One of the major problems with the decision in the *Slaughterhouse Cases* was that it suggested that the Civil War Amendments actually gave the federal government very little power to protect the rights of black Americans from state and local governments. In 1883, in a complex and technical series of cases known to historians as the *Civil Rights Cases,* the

Justices let the other shoe drop. In effect, the Supreme Court told black Americans that they were on their own. They should not look to the federal authorities for help in protecting their rights.

Exhausted by his tenure as Chief Justice, Salmon P. Chase died in 1873 after only nine years in office. President Grant appointed the able, hard-working Morrison R. Waite of Michigan to succeed Chase. Waite battled the Justices' rising workload until he himself died, in 1888.

Waite's successor, Melville W. Fuller of Maine, decided to do something about the flood of cases that was wearing out the Supreme Court Justices and federal district judges. (The rising tide of federal litigation resulted from the growth of the national economy and the legal profession, and from the development of new kinds of lawsuits and business deals.) Fuller led the Justices in lobbying Congress. In 1891, Congress passed a new Judiciary Act that reshaped the federal court system. The Act created a whole new set of federal circuit courts and authorized the appointment of dozens of new circuit court judges to staff those courts. Congress finally abolished the century-old practice of circuit riding, which had exasperated and exhausted every Supreme Court Justice from John Jay on.

The last half of the nineteenth century was marked by a major shift in the emphases of American constitutional law. During the years before the Civil War, the part of the American economy devoted to industry became more and more important. So, too, did those parts of the economy that carried out business across state lines. Industry and "interstate commerce" became a principal source of the nation's wealth. The growth of industry and interstate commerce carried with it new questions of law that sooner or later had to come before the Supreme Court.

At the same time, new ideas as to how the American economy should work were gaining popularity. In the 1873

Slaughterhouse Cases, Justices Stephen J. Field and Joseph P. Bradley emerged as spokesmen (together with many industrialists and economists) for the doctrine of *laissez faire. Laissez faire* is a French phrase meaning "leave it alone." People who believe in *laissez faire* argue that the economy works best when it is left alone to be a *free market*—that is, when buyers and sellers can do business with one another without having to worry about government regulations. Justice Field kept up the fight and began to win other members of the Supreme Court to his views.

In 1877, the case of *Munn v. Illinois* signaled a turning point in the development of constitutional rules governing state power to regulate the economy. The Illinois legislature had adopted a law regulating the rates that operators of grain storage facilities could charge farmers who wanted to store their grain while waiting for railroads to pick it up for shipment and sale in the East. The Justices upheld the Illinois law by the narrowest vote—five to four. Chief Justice Waite ruled that when an economic venture, like a grain storage facility, affects the *public interest,* the state can pass laws regulating it. But the laws had to be reasonably designed to promote the public interest. Justice Field dissented, putting forth his usual *laissez faire* arguments.

Advocates of *laissez faire* were horrified that the Court had upheld a law permitting a state to tell a private businessman how much he could charge for his services. But *Munn* allowed the Court to strike down state laws regulating economic activities that the Justices felt were *unreasonable* or that they believed did *not* advance the public interest. The Justices believed that simply taking Peter's property to give it to Paul was not a reasonable law. Nor did it advance the public interest.

As the nineteenth century came to an end, the Justices more and more often ruled against federal and state laws regulating the economy. The Court informed Congress that because manufacturing (in the Justices' view) took place within one state, it was not "interstate commerce" that Congress could regulate. The Court also declared that a federal income tax, which had been adopted as an emergency measure during the Civil War and revived in the 1890s, was a "direct tax" forbidden by the Constitution.

Many law professors, political scientists, historians, lawyers, and politicians began to attack the Court for defending the established economic system under the guise of protecting the Constitution. Once again, the Supreme Court found itself at the heart of public controversy.

The Court was not *all* serious business in this period. It is hard to imagine the Justices keeping straight faces about one of their 1890 cases: *In re Neagle*. Although a murder was at the heart of this case, it had elements of low comedy bordering on farce.

The story of *In re Neagle* had begun nearly thirty years earlier. Before President Lincoln named Stephen Field to the Supreme Court, Field had been Chief Justice of the California Supreme Court. The previous California Chief Justice was David Terry. Terry was presiding over the court when a beautiful young woman presented her case. She claimed that she had been living with a wealthy Californian as his wife for many years before he died. Somehow they had forgotten to go through the marriage ceremony. She argued that she was what lawyers call the man's "common-law" wife and thus entitled under California law to half of his property as his widow. But, she sobbed, the man's relatives claimed that she was nothing but a floozy trying to cash in on the estate of a man who had supported her handsomely while he lived.

Chief Justice Terry fell in love with the young woman—or with the money she claimed she was entitled to—and resigned from the bench to become her husband *and* her lawyer. Field succeeded him as Chief Justice. Rumors spread that the court would rule against the new Mrs. Terry. Terry publicly swore that he would "get" Field. When Field was ready to announce the court's decision, he ordered the court's marshal to search Terry. The marshal found two pistols, knives, and other weapons. Field ordered Terry thrown out of the courtroom. The decision did indeed go against the newlyweds, and Terry vowed vengeance.

When Field became an Associate Justice of the U.S. Supreme Court, in 1863, he explained the Terry matter to President Lincoln. The President assigned a federal marshal to accompany Justice Field whenever he had to ride circuit in California. More than twenty years passed, but neither Justice Field nor the Terrys forgot the vow.

On the fateful day that gave rise to *In re Neagle*, Justice Field was riding circuit in California. He was having breakfast in a railroad dining car with his current U.S. Marshal, a man named Neagle. Coincidentally, Mr. and Mrs. Terry had boarded the train, and Terry recognized Field. He strode up to Field and struck him across the face. He then reached into his own coat. Neagle later testified that he had spotted a gun under Terry's coat. The Marshal calmly pulled out *his* revolver and shot Terry dead, then went on with his breakfast. Hearing the shot, Mrs. Terry ran into the dining car and threw herself on her husband's body, sobbing hysterically. When she was removed from the scene, a search of the corpse disclosed no gun.

Neagle was arrested and tried for murder under California law. (Mrs. Terry had unsuccessfully begged the California authorities to arrest Justice Field as well.) Neagle defended himself on the ground that he was a federal officer carrying out his lawful duty in an appropriate manner. The case reached the U.S. Supreme Court. It voted, eight to zero, to accept Neagle's argument and throw out the California murder indictment. Justice Field took no part in the decision of the case. In his memoirs, he could not conceal his satisfaction at Terry's fate.

CHAPTER FIVE

THE GREAT DISSENTERS

For most of our history, the Supreme Court has been a quiet, little-noticed institution. Most of its cases have been dry and technical. As a result, until our own time, neither the public nor the press paid much attention to most of the cases decided by the Justices.

Occasionally, however, one of the Justices cannot go along with the majority and writes an explanation of his or her views. This written explanation is called a *dissenting opinion* or a *dissent.* Other Justices in the minority can join the dissenting Justice's opinion or write dissents of their own. Still others can write opinions explaining why they agree with the majority but how they got to the same result by a different route. These are called *concurring opinions* or *concurrences.*

Chief Justice Charles Evans Hughes once explained, in a book he wrote about the Court in the 1920s, that a dissenting opinion was "an appeal to the brooding omnipresence of the law." A dissenting opinion is a Justice's way to put his or her ideas before the nation, to get them thought about and discussed. A dissenting Justice hopes, often with good reason, that a later group of Justices may see the question his or her way and *overturn* the earlier decision of the Supreme Court. In this way, dissenting opinions help to shape the development of our constitutional law.

Some dissents are so eloquent or controversial that they attract the attention of the press and the public. Several Supreme Court Justices became public heroes because of their dissenting opinions. These Justices have been called "the great dissenters."

Justice John Marshall Harlan wrote one of the first and most famous great dissenting opinions in the 1896 case of *Plessy v. Ferguson*. This case challenged a Louisiana law requiring separate railroad cars for black and white passengers. The Southern states in the years after the Civil War had adopted laws, known as *Jim Crow laws*, designed to restrict the rights of black Americans. Southern legislators argued that it was necessary to adopt systems of separation, also called *segregation*, to keep peace between whites and blacks.

A lawyer named Albion W. Tourgée worked long and hard in this period to stand up for the rights of black Americans. He hated the segregation laws and came up with a way to challenge them in court. He got Homer Plessy, a black citizen of Louisiana, to sit in a whites-only railroad car. When the conductor challenged the man's right to sit in the car, Plessy quietly submitted to arrest, as Tourgée had planned. Plessy then challenged the Louisiana segregation law because it violated his right to the equal protection of the laws under the Fourteenth Amendment to the U.S. Constitution.

Tourgée's strategy backfired. The Supreme Court upheld the segregation law by a vote of eight to one. Justice Henry B. Brown wrote for the Court that segregation was not necessarily a violation of the Fourteenth Amendment's Equal Protection Clause. All that the clause required, Justice Brown declared, was that black and white citizens have access to equal facilities. *Separate* facilities could be *equal* facilities. In fact, as long as the facilities were equal, separation was not only constitutional, it also was good policy. Justice Brown doubted that black and white Americans could ever live together in peace and friendship.

Justice Harlan's was the only dissenting vote. He declared that segregation was inherently unequal. He pointed out, in one of the most famous sentences ever written by a member of the Supreme Court, "Our Constitution is color-blind." Harlan's dissenting opinion startled many Americans who never would have expected Harlan to think that way. He had been born and raised in Kentucky, a border state. He had owned slaves before the Civil War. When the war broke out, he declared his loyalty to the Union, freed his slaves, and served bravely in the Union Army. Harlan's views stung the consciences of some Americans, but he did not live to see them become the law of the land. He died in 1911, more than forty years before the Supreme Court rejected the *Plessy* doctrine of "separate but equal."

In 1902, President Theodore Roosevelt appointed a second "great dissenter" to the Supreme Court. Oliver Wendell Holmes, Jr., was born in Massachusetts in 1841, the son of a great poet and literary figure, Dr. Oliver Wendell Holmes. The younger Holmes graduated from Harvard College and served in the Union Army in the Civil War. The Justice enjoyed telling the following story about his war service: When President Lincoln once visited the front lines and was caught standing in the open as the Confederate army opened fire, young Captain Holmes bellowed at the President, "Get down, you old fool!" Holmes himself was wounded three times. When his tour of duty ended, he returned home to study law at Harvard Law School. After several years in private practice as a lawyer, he became a law professor at Harvard, then a member of the Massachusetts Supreme Judicial Court, and eventually Chief Justice of that court.

Justice Holmes was a great legal scholar. His book *The*

COLLECTION OF THE SUPREME COURT OF THE UNITED STATES

Oliver Wendell Holmes, Jr., who served as an Associate Justice for twenty-nine years (1902–1931), was the greatest legal thinker to sit on the Supreme Court. His dissenting opinions inspired generations of lawyers and public servants.

Common Law (1881) is one of the most influential books on legal history and legal thought ever published in the English-speaking world. He declared on the book's first page that "the life of the law has not been logic—it has been experience." By this observation, which Holmes backed up through several hundred pages of careful research and argument, he showed that the law is not some mystical constellation of ideas, waiting somewhere in space for judges to discover its terms. Rather, it is a growing and living thing that judges and legislators must adapt to changing problems and circumstances. These ideas sound natural to us today, for we live in the shadow of Justice Holmes. In the 1880s and 1890s, however, they were revolutionary ideas that changed the way

that judges and legal scholars thought about law for generations.

Justice Holmes brought to the U.S. Supreme Court his
remarkable store of legal knowledge and his equally remarkable knack for writing short, eloquent, pithy opinions. He
gathered around him the brightest young minds in politics
and government. Judge Learned Hand was a cherished friend.
So was Louis D. Brandeis, the crusading Boston reformer and
the best lawyer in the United States. And so was Holmes's
protégé and disciple, the young Professor Felix Frankfurter of
Harvard Law School.

Professor Frankfurter sent Justice Holmes a new Harvard
Law School graduate each year. This young man—they were
male and unmarried, by the rules of the Court at that time—
served as Justice Holmes's secretary and research assistant, or
"law clerk." Many of Justice Holmes's law clerks went on to
become leaders of the legal profession, distinguished law
professors, and judges. (This system remains today. "Clerk-
ing" for a Supreme Court Justice is a prestigious position,
sought by top law students after graduation.)

Justice Holmes disliked his colleagues' attempts to read
their personal views into the Constitution. He argued that
the people and their elected representatives had a right to run
the government in any way they saw fit as long as it did not
clearly violate the Constitution. He reminded the Justices
over and over again that the word *unconstitutional* does not
mean *unwise*. The Supreme Court should not strike down
laws that were merely silly or half-baked or poorly drafted.
The power of judicial review, Holmes taught, should be used
sparingly. *That* was the way to preserve the Court's prestige
and authority. It was also the way to make certain that the
government of the United States and the government of each
state would be democratic and not dominated by a group of
unelected judges.

Chief Justice Fuller understood and tolerated Holmes's

dissents. When Fuller died in 1910, his successor, Edward D. White of Louisiana, also understood and accepted Holmes's need to express his views. Chief Justice White had fought as a Confederate soldier. His appointment, by President William Howard Taft, an Ohioan, was seen as a symbolic gesture linking North and South. The two Civil War veterans, Chief Justice White and Justice Holmes, enjoyed talking over their memories of the war and speculating on whether they had faced each other in battle.

In 1916, fourteen years after the appointment of Justice Holmes, President Woodrow Wilson stunned the nation and the legal community by naming Holmes's friend Louis D. Brandeis to the Supreme Court. Brandeis was the first Jewish nominee to the Supreme Court. He had made many enemies because he placed his brilliant legal mind at the service of reformers who wanted the government to regulate the economy. As was the custom in that era, Brandeis did not appear in person before the Senate Judiciary Committee to answer questions about his background and views. After a bitter confirmation fight, the Senate voted to confirm Brandeis.

Brandeis was the ideal colleague for Holmes. The two men complemented each other perfectly. Holmes was a master of philosophy; Brandeis was an unsurpassed master of economic and social facts and details. They also had close ties with Professor Felix Frankfurter, who began to send clerks for Justice Brandeis as well as for Justice Holmes.

Holmes and Brandeis joined forces on the Court. They repeatedly dissented from decisions of the Court that struck down federal and state laws regulating the economy. The pair argued that those laws *were* constitutional. Brandeis explained that the states were "laboratories of reform," which had the authority under the Constitution to experiment with new ways to solve society's problems. Their opinions were publicized and quoted across the nation and found respectful hearings in the nation's foremost law schools.

In the years during and after the First World War, several cases concerning issues of free speech reached the Supreme Court for the first time. The federal government and many of the states had passed laws restricting what people could say or publish in criticizing government policy. Some of these laws were based on the lawmakers' fears of violent revolution, like the Bolshevik Revolution in November 1917 that had imposed a Communist government on Russia.

One day in 1918, a man named Abrams and several of his friends wrote, printed, and distributed handbills urging young men not to take part in the draft of men to become soldiers in the U.S. Army. The handbills were written in Yiddish and thus could not be read by most of their intended audience. Abrams and his friends threw the handbills out of open windows in office buildings in lower Manhattan; only a few reached the people they were written for. Even so, the United States prosecuted Abrams and his friends for the crime of *sedition* under a new Sedition Act enacted that year. The four were found guilty and sentenced to be *deported*—that is, shipped out of the country.

The U.S. Supreme Court had already upheld the Sedition Act in an opinion written by Justice Holmes in 1918. In *Schenck v. United States*, Holmes had declared, "The most stringent protection of free speech would not protect a man who falsely shouted fire in a crowded theatre, causing a panic." Justice Holmes believed that he had marked out a clear line between most kinds of speech, which *were* protected by the First Amendment, and the single type of speech that the government could outlaw and punish: speech that clearly threatened to cause immediate action to break the law and endanger the nation.

Although Holmes and Brandeis had helped to uphold the Sedition Act, they were appalled by the majority decision in *Abrams v. United States*. They did not believe that Abrams's actions, or those of his friends, had posed a serious threat of immediate peril to the nation, so they agreed to dissent from the majority opinion. Justice Holmes wrote a noble dissent for himself and Justice Brandeis: "The ultimate good desired is better reached by free trade in ideas. . . . The best test of truth is the power of the thought to get itself accepted in the competition of the market, and . . . truth is the only ground upon which [people's] wishes [for "the ultimate good"] safely can be carried out. That at any rate is the theory of our Constitution." Justice Holmes spelled out one more time, as clearly as he could, what kind of speech was *not* protected under the First Amendment: "It is only the present danger of an immediate evil or an intent to bring it about that warrants Congress in setting a limit to the expression of opinion where private rights are not involved."

For half a century, the Court did not heed the Holmes-Brandeis dissent in *Abrams*. Indeed, in 1925, in the case of *Gitlow v. New York,* it proposed another test for illegal speech: whether the speech in question had a "bad tendency." This is an extremely vague test, and Holmes and Brandeis joined in attacking it. But there was one feature of the *Gitlow* case that made it a landmark in our constitutional law: For the first time, the Court held that the Fourteenth Amendment imposed at least some of the terms of the U.S. Bill of Rights to limit the powers of state and local governments.

Holmes and Brandeis continued their lonely crusade to protect both individual freedom and the government's power to pass laws to solve social and economic problems. They vexed and infuriated the new Chief Justice, former President William Howard Taft, who went on the bench in 1921. (Ironically, Taft was succeeding the late Chief Justice White, whom he had appointed Chief Justice eleven years earlier. To become Chief Justice had been the greatest ambition and dream of Taft's life. Taft is the only person to be President and a Justice.) Fearful that more liberal judges would rise to the Court, the conservative Taft put enormous pressure on

President Warren G. Harding to appoint only those judges whom Taft himself approved. Thus, Taft managed to block the appointments to the Supreme Court of Learned Hand, another of Holmes's friends, and Benjamin N. Cardozo, the Chief Judge of the New York Court of Appeals.

In 1925, Justice Harlan Fiske Stone joined the Court and entered the ranks of the "great dissenters." Born in Vermont and educated with the young Calvin Coolidge at Amherst College in Massachusetts, Stone had become a distinguished legal scholar. He was Dean of Columbia Law School when President Coolidge appointed him Attorney General and ordered him to investigate the scandals left over from the Administration of the late President Warren G. Harding. President Coolidge rewarded Stone's vigorous efforts to clean up the "Teapot Dome" scandals with a seat on the Supreme Court. Stone soon infuriated Chief Justice Taft by joining Holmes and Brandeis.

Still another case where the "great dissenters" spoke over the heads of their colleagues to the nation and the future involved both a pressing legal problem and a new way to fight crime. In 1920, the Eighteenth Amendment had become part of the Constitution. This new provision banned the sale or interstate transportation of alcoholic beverages. It is popularly known as Prohibition. For over ten years, the federal government had fought a grim and determined battle against illegal manufacturers of liquor in the United States and smugglers of liquor brought in from Canada, Mexico, and Europe. One of the new weapons the government used against these bootleggers was the *wiretap*, by which the government could listen in on bootleggers' telephone conversations.

In a case that reached the Supreme Court in 1928, a bootlegger named Olmstead challenged the introduction into evidence at his trial of transcripts from a government wiretap. He declared that the government had violated his rights under the Fourth Amendment by tapping his phone and "bugging" his place of business without a warrant. The lower courts had rejected Olmstead's argument, and the Supreme Court agreed with them. Chief Justice Taft wrote an opinion for the majority in which he argued that the Fourth Amendment prohibited only "unreasonable searches and seizures." He declared that installing a wiretap or bugging device was not a "search" and that information gathered by a wiretap or bugging device was not "seized" in a way that the Fourth Amendment covered.

Justices Holmes and Brandeis again dissented. Holmes wrote a short opinion declaring wiretapping and bugging to be a "dirty business" and endorsing the reasoning of his friend Brandeis. Brandeis produced perhaps his most important judicial opinion—a long, scholarly, eloquent explanation and defense of the right to privacy, "the right most valued by civilized men." Justice Brandeis pointed out that all sorts of technological devices might be invented that could not have been imagined in 1789 by the framers of the Fourth Amendment but would destroy the right to privacy that the Revolutionary generation of Americans sought to protect. He also pointed out that government should not break the law in order to enforce it. If government did break the law (the Constitution) to enforce the law (Prohibition), Brandeis warned, the government would "invite contempt for law" throughout the society. It would thus destroy the rule of law. It took decades for Brandeis's point of view to persuade a later group of Justices. The 1928 *Olmstead* case was not overruled by the Supreme Court until *Katz v. United States* (1967) was decided.

There were some subjects that the nine Justices did agree on. In 1925, the Court, led by Chief Justice Taft, lobbied Congress for yet another Judiciary Act. The 1925 Judiciary Act was nicknamed "the Judges' Bill" because the Justices of the Supreme Court took an active role in getting Congress to adopt it. This law gave the Supreme Court control over the kinds of cases that it had to hear.

Previously, the Court had had to hear any case that fit within the law defining the Court's *appellate jurisdiction*—that is, the Court's power to hear certain kinds of cases brought to it from lower courts. The Judges' Bill created a procedure by which the Justices could decide which cases they would or would not hear. Except for a narrow class of cases, most people who want the Court to take their case have to file a request with the Court, explaining why their case is important enough for the Court to hear it. This request is called a *petition for a writ of certiorari*. At least four Justices must agree that a case is important enough for the Court to take it by issuing this writ.

The Judges' Bill also adjusted the structure of the federal court system to the shape it has today. At the lowest level, the trial courts are the U.S. District Courts. At the intermediate level are the U.S. Courts of Appeals. At the top of the pyramid is the U.S. Supreme Court.

Still another subject that the Justices could agree on was that their quarters were too small. While the President had the White House and Congress had the Capitol, the Supreme Court had to be content for most of its history with the small, overcrowded Old Senate Chamber in the depths of the Capitol. Chief Justice Taft and his colleagues persuaded Congress to consider building a new structure just for the Court.

Chief Justice Taft never lived to see the building completed; he died in 1930. His successor, Charles Evans Hughes, led the Court into the magnificent Supreme Court Building, which opened, gleaming with marble, in 1935. One Justice supposedly remarked, "By Heaven, we'll be nine black beetles in the Temple of Karnak!"

CHAPTER SIX

CHARLES EVANS HUGHES

The cast of characters of our story experienced several important changes between 1930 and 1933. Old faces departed, and new faces joined the company. These changes are important because they fashioned a critical stage in the life of the Supreme Court and our constitutional system.

When Chief Justice Taft died in early 1930, he left behind a massive legacy—a Supreme Court dominated by conservative Justices who, he knew, would defend rights of private property against experiments by federal, state, or local governments. Taft himself had appointed a few of these men during his Presidency. As a former President, he also had had tremendous influence with Presidents Harding and Coolidge on the subject of judicial appointments. But Taft would not have been pleased by the man the new President, Herbert Hoover, had chosen to succeed him.

Charles Evans Hughes had had a distinguished career in politics, law, and diplomacy. He had been an enlightened Governor of New York. President Taft had appointed him to the Supreme Court in 1910. He resigned his office in 1916 to become the Republican Party's near-victorious Presidential candidate in 1916 against President Woodrow Wilson (Hughes has been the only Supreme Court Justice to be a major party's Presidential nominee). From 1921 to 1929, he served Presidents Harding and Coolidge as one of our finest Secretaries of State. Some liberal Senators, such as the old Progressive George W. Norris of Nebraska, opposed Hughes's nomination to the Court because they believed that the former Wall Street lawyer was a tool of big business. Norris later apologized publicly to the new Chief Justice.

Hughes was a tall, imposing man with a flowing white beard. Some lawyers said that he looked the way they had always imagined God to look. He presided over the Court with dignity and firmness. He was a perfectionist who was so strict about the time limits on lawyers' arguments before the Court that he once stopped a lawyer in the middle of the word *if*. He commanded the respect of all the other members of the Court except for crusty old James McReynolds.

No one could abide McReynolds, whom President Wilson had named to the Court in 1914. McReynolds hated Jews, blacks, women, and any man who disagreed with him. He refused to sit next to Justice Brandeis on the bench or even when the Justices posed for their annual photograph. Hughes must have sighed more than once, thinking about his prickly, acid-tongued colleague.

The Chief Justice also had difficulty with McReynolds's three allies—George Sutherland, Pierce Butler, and Willis Van Devanter. These four conservative Justices were determined to uphold Chief Justice Taft's legacy of respect for the rights of private property. They consistently voted to strike down federal and state laws regulating the economy and providing government help to those in need. Reporters dubbed them the "Four Horsemen of the Apocalypse." The name comes from the New Testament's *Book of the Revelation of St. John,* which describes Pestilence, War, Famine, and

Death as four horsemen taking part in the final confrontation between Good and Evil.

A Justice who had voted frequently with Taft and the "Four Horsemen" died on the very same day that Taft died. Justice Edward Sanford was known as "Taft's shadow" because he had been recommended by Taft, had always voted with Taft, and now had died with Taft. President Hoover appointed Owen J. Roberts to succeed Sanford. Roberts was a moderate who shunned the extremes of liberalism and conservatism. He kept his own counsel, but his fellow Justices soon realized that they should not underestimate him. The quiet Roberts would make a difference when he chose to.

A second change of personnel on the Court meant the departure of one of the giants of American law. Justice Holmes had turned ninety in 1931. Chief Justice Hughes every now and then had had to nudge him awake during oral arguments. Holmes finally admitted that he was too old to continue in office and wrote out a brief letter of resignation in January 1932. He lived four more years, dying in early 1935, a beloved figure and one of the giants of the law.

President Hoover had the task of appointing Holmes's successor. He looked at one name on the list over and over again—Chief Judge Benjamin Nathan Cardozo of the New York Court of Appeals. Cardozo was Jewish, Hoover knew, and so was Justice Brandeis. The President worried whether the country would tolerate two Jewish Supreme Court Justices serving at the same time. But he also knew that the legal community unanimously considered Cardozo to be the greatest judge in the United States. He finally decided that the country needed Cardozo on the Court. Instead of the outcry he expected, the President was deluged with praise for the appointment by everybody, including former Justice Holmes. Only Justice McReynolds disapproved. He read a newspaper during Cardozo's swearing-in ceremony to show the world what *he* thought of the matter.

COLLECTION OF THE SUPREME COURT OF THE UNITED STATES

*The Hughes Court in 1931, with the "Great Dissenters" (GD)
and the "Four Horsemen" (FH): left to right, standing, Harlan
Fiske Stone (GD), George Sutherland (FH), Pierce Butler (FH),
Owen J. Roberts; left to right, sitting, James C. McReynolds (FH),
Oliver W. Holmes, Jr. (GD), Chief Justice Charles Evans Hughes,
Willis Van Devanter (FH), Louis D. Brandeis (GD).*

Cardozo was a quiet, gentle man who looked far older than
his sixty-two years. His father, Judge Albert Cardozo of the
New York State Supreme Court, had been forced off the
bench in disgrace when investigations disclosed that he had
been a party to the corruption of New York City's "Tammany
Hall" Democratic organization. Young Benjamin was perma-
nently scarred by his father's disgrace. He never married and
never showed any interest in anything but the law. He had a
distinguished record in college and law school at Columbia
University and soon stepped forward as a successful reform
candidate for a New York City Civil Court judgeship. Cardozo

soon won election to the state's highest court, the Court of Appeals (New York State's Supreme Court is actually its trial court), and then became Chief Judge of that court. He was famous throughout the nation and the rest of the Western world for his scholarship and his elegant writing style. His lectures and essays about jurisprudence, which were published as *The Nature of the Judicial Process*, *The Growth of the Law*, *Paradoxes of Legal Science*, and *Law and Literature*, are classics of the philosophy of law. He succeeded Holmes as a member of the liberal bloc on the Court, with Justices Brandeis and Stone.

President Hoover was defeated for re-election in 1932 by Democrat Franklin D. Roosevelt, a towering figure in the history of American politics. Hoover was the victim of the American people's desire for a government that would do *something* about the Great Depression, which had begun in 1929, and of the people's demand for the repeal of the Eighteenth Amendment (Prohibition).

President Roosevelt was determined to experiment with government to combat the Depression and aid Americans in want. He was not afraid to propose government programs that President Hoover had felt might violate the Constitution. In 1933, Congress and the American people were eager to back up anything that President Roosevelt suggested. Congress even voted to adopt New Deal laws that many of its members had not read through. Many of these laws had been poorly drafted, however, and some of them were clearly unconstitutional. Court cases challenging these laws began to make their way up the federal judicial ladder.

The most famous of these cases was brought by the Schechter Poultry Corporation. The Schechter brothers, who ran a chicken business in New York City, found themselves confronted by the centerpiece of the first New Deal laws: the National Industrial Recovery Act, which created the National Recovery Administration (NRA), symbolized by the famous "blue eagle." The NRA was based on the idea that economic competition was a major reason for the Depression. Competition caused rival companies to undercut each other to win more business. Runaway price cutting and massive employee layoffs had indeed helped to bring about the Depression. The NRA organized each industry, including the poultry industry, and authorized the leading companies in each industry to issue a code, or set of rules, that governed prices, quality of product, and other matters. The codes had the force of law. The poultry industry accused the Schechter brothers of violating the poultry industry code—specifically by selling sick chickens. The Schechters decided to fight the government's attempt to prosecute them.

The "sick chicken" case (as it became known) reached the Supreme Court in 1935. The Justices were unanimous in their decision for the Schechters and against the NRA. Even liberals Brandeis, Cardozo, and Stone went along. (In fact, even before the case reached the federal courts, Justice Brandeis tried to warn the President that the NRA would be declared unconstitutional if it ever came before the Court. But Brandeis's message, carried by his and Roosevelt's friend Professor Felix Frankfurter, fell on deaf ears.) The NRA, the Court ruled, violated the Constitution. Congress had *delegated,* or given, its authority to make laws not just to an executive agency but to the private companies that the law authorized to write the codes for each industry. Congress could not delegate this lawmaking power to the executive branch. It certainly could not give it to private companies.

President Roosevelt secretly did not mind too much about the death of the "blue eagle" because the NRA was not bringing the economy out of the Depression. But the *Schechter* decision angered Roosevelt because the Supreme Court seemed not to be interested in helping the country shake off the Depression. The President feared that the Court would cause more problems for the New Deal—and he was right.

The Justices struck down several more New Deal laws. In these cases, they were not unanimous, however. The "Four Horsemen" were able to win over Justice Roberts, and sometimes even Chief Justice Hughes, to strike down one law after another. Justices Brandeis, Cardozo, and Stone filed a series of eloquent and angry dissenting opinions, but they were cold comfort to the President. It seemed that the Court was throwing out New Deal measures almost as fast as Congress and the President could pass them.

In 1936, President Roosevelt won a smashing victory in his bid for a second term, carrying forty-six of the forty-eight states. As part of his campaign, he had attacked the conservative decisions of the Supreme Court. His landslide triumph gave him an idea: Why should the Court stand alone against the mandate that Roosevelt had won from the people?

In early 1937, Roosevelt dropped a bombshell. He gave a speech announcing that he had come up with a "Court reorganization bill." In the radio speech he delivered explaining the bill, he sought the people's backing for his proposal. The Justices, he pointed out, were old. They were not retiring because the government had no pension system that would permit them to retire. No wonder they were staying on the bench into their seventies and eighties; they had to stay active to earn money to support themselves and their families. But because they were so old and tired, the Justices could not keep up with their workload. Even more important, Roosevelt insisted, the Justices could not keep up with the changing times: "Little by little, new facts become blurred through old glasses fitted, as it were, for the needs of another generation." The Court needed help, the President declared.

President Roosevelt described a bill that he was about to send to Congress to solve the Court's problems. For every Justice over seventy who chose not to retire, Roosevelt suggested that he (the President) be allowed to appoint an additional Justice to help carry the workload of the Court.

There would be a maximum of six new justices—not by coincidence, the exact number of members of the Court over seventy.

The bill sounded simple, but the Justices realized what it was: a measure to permit the President to "pack" the Court with Justices who would support his programs. Eighty-year-old Justice Brandeis was hurt and outraged. Although he was the oldest Justice, he had also voted to support most of the New Deal laws struck down by his colleagues. Most important, he had tried repeatedly to warn the Administration to be more careful in drafting its bills. Now, it seemed, he was being punished and humiliated.

The American people also realized what the bill was designed to do. They were angered by the Court's decisions, but that did not mean that they were ready to injure the Court's independence. Many Americans thought that the Supreme Court was the equivalent of the Constitution. The President's proposal seemed to be a slap at the Constitution—a badly timed one in the Constitution's 150th year. The President discovered that he did not have the people behind him this time.

The Court-packing controversy was the first to enmesh all three branches of government in eighty years—since the *Dred Scott* case of 1857. For months, Congressional debate raged over the Court-packing bill. Democrat Joseph Robinson of Arkansas, the Majority Leader in the Senate, supported the bill—but he had set a price for his support: Roosevelt had to promise him the first new seat on the Court. Roosevelt and other liberals were not pleased with this necessary bargain. Robinson was a very conservative Democrat, and they feared he might not be faithful to the New Deal as a Justice.

Democrat Burton K. Wheeler of Montana, a leading Senatorial opponent of the Court reorganization bill, had an idea and wrote to Chief Justice Hughes. Was the Court really overworked? Was the bill necessary?

Chief Justice Hughes *was* opposed to the bill. He had grumbled to friends that "if Congress wants me to preside over a convention, I can do it." But he believed that the dignity and independence of the Court would not permit him to oppose the bill actively. Wheeler's letter presented an opportunity to work against the bill without seeming to work against it. Hughes consulted with Justice Brandeis, of the liberal bloc, and Justice Van Devanter, of the conservative Four Horsemen, on a response, which Wheeler read to the Senate.

No, the Chief Justice declared, the Court was not over-worked. In fact, it was ahead of its work at that point. Besides, he pointed out, the Court reorganization bill would actually make *more* work for the Court: There would be more Justices to consult, more to write opinions, more to decide, more to debate.

The Hughes letter took the wind out of the sails of the Court-packing plan. But Senator Robinson was stubborn. He wanted that seat on the Court. He continued to fight for the bill. Then the second shoe dropped.

In a surprise decision, the Justices upheld a major New Deal law, the National Labor Relations Act of 1935. The vote in the case of *National Labor Relations Board v. Jones & Laughlin Steel Corp.* was five to four. Justice Owen Roberts, the quiet Pennsylvanian who had previously tended to vote with the Four Horsemen, had provided the needed fifth vote to uphold the National Labor Relations Act as constitutional. Labor unions applauded, for they regarded the law as "labor's Bill of Rights." The country heaved a sigh of relief, calling Justice Roberts's vote "the switch in time that saved nine"—that is, the nine Justices. For the rest of his life, Roberts maintained that the Court-packing controversy had had nothing to do with his vote; he sincerely believed that the labor law was constitutional. But there was no doubt that his vote to uphold the law had shown that the Court would be receptive to New Deal measures that were constitutional.

The Four Horsemen were furious. Justice Sutherland, their intellectual leader, read his entire dissenting opinion from the bench. He was red-faced and angry. One reporter noticed that his remarks from the bench were even more pointed and furious than his written opinion. Everyone saw that the power of the Four Horsemen was at an end.

Two more events helped to kill the Court-packing plan. The first was the retirement of Justice Willis Van Devanter. Congress had finally provided a pension system for the Justices, and Van Devanter stepped down to take advantage of it. For the first time in his Presidency, Roosevelt had a chance to appoint a new Justice. The second event was the unexpected death of Senator Robinson, who collapsed on the floor of the Senate, still fighting for the bill and his dream of a seat on the Court.

The President decided to abandon the Court-packing bill. It was his first major defeat in Congress, and he was not happy about it. He had invested much of his energy and prestige in the bill, and he hated ending up with egg on his face. But the country was happy to see the controversy blow away, and Roosevelt realized it. Besides, he now had the opportunity to appoint Justices to the Court. Thus, he could help to reshape American constitutional law.

Chief Justice Hughes was privately delighted with the downfall of the Court-packing plan. He had managed to preserve the independence of the Court without getting it involved in the rough-and-tumble of politics, which would have destroyed the Court's independence and prestige. He had also managed to change the Court's direction so that it would not be a rigid opponent of the Administration's attempts to solve the problems of the American economic system. And he had ensured that the debate over the Court-packing bill would be a high-level debate about the Constitution and the system of government it created.

Historians have agreed that Hughes's careful statesmanship saved the Court and the Constitution's system of checks and balances. Thanks to the Chief Justice's efforts, the Supreme Court was preserved to help the nation deal with the pressing problems awaiting it in the years ahead.

CHAPTER SEVEN

PROBLEMS OF WAR
AND PEACE

In late 1937, President Roosevelt nominated his first Supreme Court Justice. He was still smarting from his defeat in the Court-packing controversy, and he wanted to "punish" the Court by appointing a hard-and-fast supporter of the bill. He also wanted to name a loyal advocate of the New Deal. And he wanted to make certain that the Senate would confirm his nominee. He chose Senator Hugo L. Black of Alabama, knowing that the Senate would be hard-pressed to turn down one of their own colleagues. He was right.

Justice Black had been born and raised in rural Alabama. He had served briefly as a police court judge and had piled up a record as a Senator who frequently used an iron hand in conducting Congressional investigations. He was an ardent New Dealer who seemed to be a truly liberal Southerner—a combination that Roosevelt thought would be ideal for the Court. Black celebrated his confirmation by taking a vacation in Europe.

Soon after Justice Black's departure, newspaper reporters stumbled over a sensational story: Justice Black had been a member of the racist Ku Klux Klan. This organization was born in the defeated South in the 1860s and 1870s, following the end of the Civil War. Dressed in white sheets and pointed hoods to hide their faces, Klansmen tarred and feathered and lynched black men who had sought to exercise their constitutional right to vote and white politicians who had tried to help the freed slaves. The original Klan had been put down by the Union Army, but the Klan had revived throughout the nation in the 1920s. The new Klansmen denounced Catholics, Jews, immigrants, and blacks with equal force and nastiness. The Klan had been a major issue in the Democratic conventions of 1924 and 1928 when Al Smith, a Catholic, denounced the Klan, and his political opponents in the party found themselves forced to tolerate the Klansmen. Now, it seemed, the white hood and sheet of the Klan were lurking under the black robes of a Supreme Court Justice.

Justice Black met the issue head-on when he returned home. In a dramatic radio address, the soft-voiced Alabaman admitted, "I *did* join the Klan." He explained that anyone who had hoped to succeed in Alabama politics—or, indeed, in politics anywhere in the South—had either to join the Klan or to agree not to oppose it. He affirmed that he was free of any kind of racial or other prejudice and pledged to the nation that he would deal fairly with Americans of any race, color, religion, or sex who came before the Supreme Court.

Despite some calls for his resignation, Justice Black stayed on the Court and proved that he had meant every word of his radio speech. He won respect as a defender of the Constitutional rights of black Americans and as an ardent defender of freedom of religion, speech, and press.

President Roosevelt ultimately filled eight of the Court's nine seats. In 1941, when Charles Evans Hughes decided to retire, Roosevelt moved Harlan Fiske Stone up from the post of Associate Justice to succeed Hughes—a decision that pleased Hughes. Three of the other Justices appointed by

Roosevelt stand out: Felix Frankfurter, William O. Douglas, and Robert H. Jackson.

Felix Frankfurter was overwhelmed when President Roosevelt decided that he should succeed the late Justice Benjamin Cardozo, who had died in July 1938. Frankfurter had been convinced that Roosevelt would never name him to the Court because his strident advocacy of liberal causes made him far too controversial. Besides, he was Jewish, and anti-Jewish feeling in America was still widespread. But Roosevelt decided that Frankfurter belonged on the Court—both because Frankfurter was a valued friend and because he probably knew more about the Supreme Court than any other living person. The short, dynamic, eloquent Harvard Law School professor dazzled the Senate Judiciary Committee with his wide-ranging knowledge of the Court and of American constitutional law. He won confirmation easily.

Three weeks after Justice Frankfurter joined the Court in early 1939, Justice Brandeis decided it was time for him to step down. President Roosevelt appointed as his successor one of the youngest men ever to be named to the Supreme Court: forty-year-old William O. Douglas, the chairman of the Securities and Exchange Commission. Douglas had taught law at Columbia and Yale law schools, and he was renowned for his understanding of the economic system and for his mastery of difficult and technical questions of law and fact. Brandeis was delighted with Roosevelt's choice of Douglas to succeed him. Douglas was a lonely, difficult, brilliant man. He had been born in the small town of Yakima, Washington, and was imbued with the fiercely independent spirit of the Northwest.

Robert H. Jackson had been one of Roosevelt's toughest and most reliable allies in the Court-packing fight. He had been one of the greatest occupants of the office of Solicitor General—the government's chief lawyer, who supervises the government's appearances in cases in the federal courts, especially the Supreme Court. Jackson had become Attorney General, but his eye was on a seat on the Supreme Court, perhaps even the post of Chief Justice. He was miffed in 1941 when Roosevelt chose Harlan Fiske Stone to succeed Chief Justice Hughes, but the President promised Jackson the next vacancy on the Court and soon kept his promise.

Stone was a better Associate Justice than a Chief Justice. Lacking Hughes's gift for managing conflict, he could not prevent the drawing of lines between Justices Black and Douglas, on the one hand, and Justices Frankfurter and Jackson, on the other.

Frankfurter and Jackson resisted using the powers of the Court in a free-swinging fashion to vindicate individual rights. They invoked the tradition of Justices Holmes and Brandeis. The Court, they declared, was an undemocratic institution in a democratic system of government. It should use its powers only when absolutely necessary. It should not play St. George looking for dragons to kill and wrongs to right. Black and Douglas disagreed. They maintained that the Court had long ignored individuals' claims for protection for their constitutional rights. It was up to the Justices now to repair that balance.

Personal differences added venom to the differences in judicial philosophy between the Black-Douglas wing of the Court and the Frankfurter-Jackson wing. Justice Frankfurter still behaved as if he were a Harvard Law School professor. He tended to lecture his colleagues as if he were still running a constitutional law seminar at Harvard and they were backward law students. Black especially resented and resisted Frankfurter. Douglas was also irritated by Frankfurter, for he too had been a brilliant law professor and considered himself to be at least as intelligent as Frankfurter was. (These divisions persisted into the 1960s.)

As the Court entered the 1940s, it faced several thorny

cases raising issues concerning the Bill of Rights. Two sets of cases stand out.

The United States has spawned many unusual religious groups, but none more so than the Jehovah's Witnesses. One of the Witnesses' central beliefs got them into trouble repeatedly with the federal and state governments: They argued that all governments were not only illegitimate but evil. The Witnesses recognized no government but that of God. They thus refused to comply with many government requirements, such as the draft, because they refused to acknowledge the authority of government.

In the late 1930s, the Gobitis family of Minersville, Pennsylvania, got into trouble with the local school board because the family were Jehovah's Witnesses. The Gobitis children refused to salute the American flag and recite the Pledge of Allegiance because they believed that saluting the American flag was the same as worshipping an idol, which the Bible commanded against. When the children were expelled from school, their parents sued the town's board of education.

The case reached the Supreme Court in 1940. The Gobitises claimed that their freedom of religious belief under the First Amendment had been violated. The Justices ruled, eight to one, that the school board could constitutionally require pupils in school to pledge allegiance and salute the flag. Justice Frankfurter delivered the Court's opinion. He argued that in those troubled times, when Europe was falling to the forces of the Nazis in Germany and the Fascists in Italy, the government could encourage feelings of patriotism even though the measures might offend the religious views of some Americans. Justice Stone was the lone dissenter. He accepted the Gobitis family's arguments about their freedom of religion and scolded his colleagues on the Court for agreeing to encourage patriotism by means that denied the freedoms that America stood for.

The *Gobitis* case raised a major outcry. The nation's newspapers denounced the Court and Justice Frankfurter. Several of the Justices were sensitive to public opinion and began to think about whether they had made a mistake in *Gobitis*. Also, as old Justices retired and new ones joined the Court, it became clear that the Supreme Court might reconsider its holdings in *Gobitis*. And it did, within three years.

In the 1943 case of *West Virginia Board of Education v. Barnette*, the Supreme Court abandoned its earlier position in *Gobitis*. In this new case, the vote was also eight to one, but this time Justice Frankfurter found himself alone in dissent. Justice Jackson explained in his opinion for the Court that the Justices were upholding the freedom of conscience of the individual. Forcing everyone to agree on an idea, even one so noble as patriotism, achieved only "the unanimity of the graveyard." Justice Frankfurter wrote an impassioned dissenting opinion. He explained that if his purely personal views were at stake, he would of course agree with the majority. After all, he was Jewish, and the Jewish people had long been targets of persecution all over the world. But he was a Justice of the Supreme Court, and his personal views had nothing to do with his beliefs as a Justice about what was constitutional or unconstitutional.

In another civil liberties controversy, Japanese-Americans were not so lucky as the Jehovah's Witnesses. When Japan's navy and air force bombed American military bases at Pearl Harbor, Hawaii, on December 7, 1941, the United States was drawn into the Second World War. Many Americans feared— without reason—that Japanese-Americans (both those who had come here from Japan years or decades before and those who had been born in the United States) would secretly work for Japan to sabotage the American war effort. Their fears were largely the result of racial prejudice.

President Roosevelt signed Executive Order No. 9066, authorizing the War Department to take necessary measures to prevent such domestic sabotage. The War Department rounded up over 110,000 Japanese nationals and naturalized citizens living in the United States and their children, who were American citizens by birth. The Army forced them to give up their property and businesses and careers, and herded them into "relocation centers" in the Western deserts. Although these "relocation centers" were nothing like the Nazi death camps, which murdered millions of Jews, Gypsies, and others in Europe during the war, they *were* concentration camps by the definition of that term then in use throughout the world.

Several young Americans of Japanese ancestry sued in federal court to challenge the government's internment measures. The Justices upheld the measures as valid wartime acts of the federal government. It took forty years for a series of lawsuits by brave and determined lawyers to overturn this blot on American justice. Even so, in late 1987 the Supreme Court refused their pleas that the United States be required to compensate the Japanese-Americans for their lost property. In the spring of 1988, the government and the Japanese-American Citizens League were close to an agreement providing monetary compensation for the surviving internees.

Chief Justice Stone died suddenly in 1946, as he was reading a dissenting opinion from the bench. By this time, a new President was in the White House, Harry S Truman. He consulted former Chief Justice Hughes, even inviting the old man to return to the Court, but Hughes turned him down, recommending that the President appoint Justice Jackson to succeed Stone. Jackson was in Europe at the time. He was the chief American member of the Nuremberg War Crimes Tribunal, which was trying former Nazi officials for "crimes against humanity." In his absence, Justices Black and Douglas apparently took the opportunity to lobby the Administration against appointing Jackson to succeed Stone. Jackson got wind of their efforts and issued a blast of his own, vigorously denouncing Black for supposed improprieties in a case called

Jewell Ridge in which Black had not disqualified himself even though his former law partner had argued the case before the Court. The issue was far from clear-cut, and Jackson went overboard in his attack on Black. The controversy threatened to split the Court beyond repair. President Truman decided not to appoint Jackson or any other current member of the Court. Instead, he turned to his old friend and Secretary of the Treasury, Fred M. Vinson of Kentucky.

If Stone had been a weak Chief Justice, Vinson was even worse. He had been a fine Senator and a good Cabinet official, but he was at best a mediocre lawyer and judge. He was a fish out of water on the Court. The other Justices had no respect for him. One day at lunch, they discussed the possibility that there be no separate office of Chief Justice and instead that the title could rotate from Justice to Justice if the Court so chose. Vinson managed to get on well with only the three other Justices whom Truman was to appoint: Harold H. Burton of Ohio, who was praised by his colleagues and everyone else who knew him as the fairest man ever to sit on the Court; Tom Clark of Texas, a former Attorney General, whom Truman later labeled "the biggest mistake I ever made"; and Sherman Minton of Indiana, one of the most colorless men ever to sit on the Supreme Court.

The Vinson Court continued divided and quarrelsome. The Justices split repeatedly on civil liberties issues and on other vital cases. Perhaps the most important case of Vinson's Chief Justiceship emerged from the Korean Conflict (1950–1953).

At the height of the Korean Conflict, the nation's steel mills were about to be shut down by a major strike. Neither management nor labor would budge. Because uninterrupted steel production was vital to the war effort, President Truman invoked his "war powers" under the Constitution and seized the steel mills. He then drafted the steel workers into the Army and ordered them back to work. One manufacturer,

Jones & Laughlin Steel Corp., challenged the President's executive orders. The federal court system sped the case through the pipeline to get it before the Supreme Court. The Justices agreed with the steel company and declared the President's orders unconstitutional. A clear majority of the Justices rejected Truman's claims of inherent Presidential war powers: The President, they held, had invaded the legitimate powers of Congress. Truman was furious, but agreed to abide by the Court's decision. It was a major victory for the rule of law.

Under Chief Justice Vinson, the Court had to deal more and more with questions of individual rights. Congressional investigating committees and the Justice Department mounted campaigns against current and former members of the Communist Party. These men and women, government investigators charged, were secretly supporting the Soviet Union, America's adversary in the "Cold War." Targets of these investigations claimed that their activities were protected by the First Amendment from criminal punishment or from congressional harassment, but the government persisted. These individuals tried to persuade the Justices to recognize that the First Amendment protected individuals' rights to say and think as they wished and to join organizations without penalty. But most of the Justices agreed with the government that the Communist Party posed a threat to the national security. Thus, the government was free to make membership in the Communist Party a crime. The government was also free to fire a government employee for being even a former member of the Party. These issues were to persist into the 1950s.

CHAPTER EIGHT

EARL WARREN AND THE "WARREN REVOLUTION"

In the summer of 1953, Chief Justice Vinson died suddenly. The Supreme Court was in the middle of hearing arguments on a major series of cases brought by black Americans challenging state laws segregating public school systems. Vinson had been clearly unfriendly to the challengers. Justice Felix Frankfurter, who wanted the Court to strike down segregation laws as unconstitutional, had been deeply worried about Vinson's likely opposition. Frankfurter also detested Vinson. As he was dressing for the Chief Justice's funeral, Frankfurter told his law clerk that Vinson's death was the first proof he had ever had of the existence of God.

The new Republican President, Dwight D. Eisenhower, cast about for Vinson's successor. Although he had promised the first Court vacancy to Governor Earl Warren of California, he resisted naming the Governor to be Chief Justice. Warren had challenged Eisenhower for the 1952 Republican Presidential nomination; also, the two men did not like each other. Eisenhower viewed his pledge as a political consolation prize; to give Warren the Chief Justiceship was more than his due. But Warren successfully insisted that the President honor his promise.

Warren was confirmed, although liberals were distressed by the appointment because of Warren's support for harsh war-time measures against Japanese-Americans during the Second World War. But Warren, whom the Court's law clerks soon dubbed the "Superchief," amazed everyone, including the President who had appointed him, because of his deep commitment to the cause of civil rights.

Warren worked with the tireless Felix Frankfurter to ensure that all nine Justices would line up behind a decision striking down school segregation. He himself wrote a carefully phrased, deliberately low-key opinion that all the Justices could accept. And he prepared himself and his colleagues for what he expected to be a firestorm of criticism.

The Supreme Court announced its unanimous decision in *Brown v. Board of Education* on May 17, 1954. It was the first of two decisions, known to historians as *Brown I*. This opinion held that separation of blacks and whites is inherently unequal. The Court silently rejected the 1896 decision in *Plessy v. Ferguson*, which stood for the rule that separate treatment of blacks and whites does not violate the Fourteenth Amendment's requirement of "equal protection of the laws." The second case, known as *Brown II*, was announced a year later. *Brown II* dealt with the way to repair, or remedy, the wrongs resulting from the segregation systems struck down by *Brown I*. The Supreme Court ordered that desegregation take place "with all deliberate speed."

Many Southern states and cities vowed to resist *Brown*. They accused the Supreme Court of *usurping*, or stealing, power from the states. Proposals were introduced in Congress for a constitutional amendment to strip the Court of power over civil rights cases. Southern Senators delayed for nearly a year the vote to confirm President Eisenhower's nomination to the Court of federal Judge John Marshall Harlan—the grandson of the Justice who had declared in 1896 that "our Constitution is color-blind"—to succeed the late Justice Robert H. Jackson. (Jackson was the last Justice to die in office.)

But the nation agreed with Chief Justice Warren, and *Brown* was a great victory for civil rights and a landmark in our constitutional history. In 1967, the black lawyer who had led the victorious team of civil rights attorneys, Thurgood Marshall, became the first black Justice of the U.S. Supreme Court. He was appointed by President Lyndon B. Johnson, a Texan.

Brown was only the first of many cases in which Chief Justice Warren led what several historians have dubbed the "Warren Revolution." He was quickly recognized as one of the most forceful Chief Justices ever to hold the office. Under his leadership, the Supreme Court stepped forward as the guardian of individual rights and racial equality.

For example, the Warren Court ruled that Congress's power to regulate interstate commerce authorized the federal government to ban segregation in private places, such as restaurants and motels. The Court also applied federal constitutional standards to the rules that states used to define the rights of people accused of crimes. The Justices ruled that the Fourth Amendment to the Constitution, which prohibits "unreasonable searches and seizures" of private homes, restricts the powers of state and local governments as well as the federal government. They held that a person accused of a serious crime who is too poor to afford a lawyer has a right to a lawyer appointed by and paid by the government, because of the Sixth Amendment to the Constitution. They limited the powers of the federal and state governments to punish persons for left-wing political views. They argued over the limits on the government's power to regulate or prohibit pornography and whether pornography is protected by the First Amendment's guarantees of freedom of the press. They reminded the states that the First Amendment's religion clauses protect

COLLECTION OF THE SUPREME COURT OF THE UNITED STATES

These nine men—the Warren Court—were the center of swirling nationwide controversy and attacks in the mid-1960s: left to right, standing, Abe Fortas, Potter Stewart, Byron R. White, Thurgood Marshall (the first black to sit on the Court); left to right, sitting, John Marshall Harlan, Hugo L. Black, Chief Justice Earl Warren, William O. Douglas, William J. Brennan, Jr.

separation of church and state, and they struck down laws and rules requiring prayer or Bible reading in the public schools.

Chief Justice Warren declared that the most important decisions of the Warren Court had to do with the way that states run elections for their legislatures. State legislatures divide the states into legislative districts, a process called *apportionment.* Often, the people in charge of drawing the borders of these districts have tried to make sure that they will stay in power. They have drawn boundaries giving the people of a large city the same number of representatives in the state legislature as a handful of people in a rural county. They have made certain that black voters are underrepresented in state and local legislatures.

In 1963, the Supreme Court struck down Tennessee's apportionment of its state legislature, which watered down the votes of the people of Memphis, the state's largest city. The Court declared that the Constitution embodies a principle of "one person, one vote." States must ensure that their legislative districts are so marked out that this principle is a reality.

Again, controversy raged. Again, many politicians called for a constitutional amendment cutting back the powers of the Supreme Court. They were joined by some legal scholars who were concerned about what the Court was doing. These scholars agreed with Justice Felix Frankfurter. They taught that the Court is not a democratic branch of government; if it were too eager to strike down laws passed by democratically elected federal and state legislatures or actions ordered by democratically elected federal and state executives, the Court would be in danger of losing its authority and prestige. They also worried that a too-active Supreme Court would cause people to forget how to govern themselves through the democratic processes of legislation and elections.

The defenders of the Warren Court replied that the democratic branches of government had been far too slow to act to defend individual rights and racial equality. It took the Court to win these victories and to make the elected officials of the federal and state governments live up to their responsibilities to all Americans. The Court was merely acting as the conscience of the nation. The debate continues to this day.

Some right-wing Americans mounted a demand to impeach Chief Justice Warren. Some even accused him of being a Communist agent. Warren chose to ignore these charges. He did his best to give effect to the fundamental values that he believed were at the heart of the Constitution even when the text did not state them clearly.

On November 22, 1963, President John F. Kennedy was shot and killed as he rode in a motorcade in Dallas, Texas. As the country reeled, the new President, Lyndon B. Johnson, appointed a commission to investigate the assassination. He asked Chief Justice Warren to preside over the commission. Warren at first did not want to accept. He believed that the Chief Justice had a responsibility to the nation and the Court that could not be put aside. Eventually, he gave in to the President, for he believed that the crisis was so special and the need to reassure the nation so great that he had to put aside his other obligations.

The Warren Commission worked for nearly a year. Its *Report* declared that a lone gunman, Lee Harvey Oswald, had slain the President for reasons unknown and that Oswald's murder two days later by Jack Ruby, a Dallas nightclub owner, was a bizarre crime by a loner. The Warren Commission *Report* sparked a controversy that still is lively decades later. Chief Justice Warren publicly and privately refused to specu-late on the web of conspiracy theories that still surrounds the case.

The most famous Warren Court decision may well be *Miranda v. Arizona,* handed down in 1966. In this case, Chief Justice Warren first spelled out the substance of the famous "Miranda warnings" that police officers must read to criminal suspects before questioning them:

> You have the right to remain silent. If you choose to give up the right to remain silent, anything you say can be used in evidence in a court of law. You have the right to have an attorney present during questioning. If you so desire, or cannot afford one, an attorney will be appointed for you by the court.

The Chief Justice believed that these warnings were the best way to make sure that suspects knew their rights under the

Constitution. At first, police officers resented the *Miranda* decision, but in recent years they have accepted it because it makes police officers better at their job. (If the police follow the guidelines in *Miranda,* they guard against the possibility that a court will throw out a case because a defendant's rights were violated.)

When Earl Warren determined to retire in 1968, President Johnson tried to promote an old friend, Justice Abe Fortas, to become the nation's first Jewish Chief Justice. Conservative Senators blocked the appointment, asking harsh questions about Fortas's financial dealings. Fortas withdrew his name and, within two years, was forced to resign from the Court. Warren had to remain as Chief Justice until Johnson's successor, President Richard M. Nixon, appointed Judge Warren E. Burger of Minnesota as the nation's fifteenth Chief Justice, in the summer of 1969. Nixon and Warren, both Californians, had detested each other since 1952, when Nixon abandoned Warren's campaign for the Republican Presidential nomination to back Dwight Eisenhower, who rewarded Nixon with the Vice Presidential nomination. Nixon had won the Presidency in 1968 running on a "law-and-order" ticket that had harshly criticized the Warren Court's decisions on the rights of criminal suspects. Thus, it was ironic that President Nixon nominated Chief Justice Warren's successor.

When Earl Warren left office, most of the criticism of the Warren Revolution abated. He died in 1974, mourned by the entire nation. He will live on as a symbol of the idea that the law should be responsive to the powerless and the weak in our society, and that judges should be able to use the law creatively to help prod society and government into solving major social problems.

CHAPTER NINE

THE BURGER COURT

Federal Judge Warren E. Burger of Minnesota was known as a tough-minded conservative—precisely what President Nixon wanted the new Chief Justice to be. Nixon dubbed Burger a *strict constructionist*—a judge who reads and applies the Constitution as written, rather than one who tries to find new rights lurking in the language of the document.

When Justice Fortas resigned in 1970, President Nixon wanted to name a strict constructionist Justice who would cement Southern support for his Administration. But his nominee, federal Judge Clement Haynsworth of South Carolina, ran into trouble. Liberal Senators accused him of having been a member of segregated social clubs and of financial misconduct. Haynsworth was defeated by the Senate. Nixon tried again, naming Judge G. Harrold Carswell of Florida, but Carswell also was defeated. Even moderate Republicans could not stomach a nominee who had a clear record of racist and pro-segregation activity in the 1940s and 1950s. Finally, Nixon appointed Judge Harry A. Blackmun of Minnesota, a childhood acquaintance of Chief Justice Burger and an able federal appellate judge. Blackmun answered reporters' questions whether he was a "strict constructionist" by saying, "I don't know what that means." (Burger and Blackmun were briefly dubbed "the Minnesota Twins.")

Some constitutional scholars hailed the Burger Court as a sign that the days of the free-wheeling Warren Court were over. Others fretted that the new Chief Justice would lead a wholesale attack on the landmarks of the Warren era. Neither side proved to be correct. The Burger Court consolidated advances made by the Warren Court—trimming some Warren Court precedents and reasserting others. In fact, some Burger Court decisions went beyond anything expected from the Warren Court.

In 1971, a former Pentagon employee, Dr. Daniel Ellsberg, decided to act against U.S. involvement in the Vietnam Conflict. He had helped to write a secret Defense Department history of decision making in that war. Now, he decided he would leak his copy of that history to The New York Times. The Times began publishing a series of articles in the spring of that year. Its page-one exclusives were accompanied by extensive extracts from the "Pentagon Papers," including secret government documents. When the government, through Attorney General John Mitchell, tried to suppress further publication of the Pentagon Papers, the Times decided to fight. So, too, did the Washington Post, to whom Ellsberg leaked the history after a federal court in New York City issued an order blocking the Times from publishing more excerpts from the history. When the government sought to restrain the Post, the Boston Globe began its own series. The story spread beyond the government's power to choke it off.

The case reached the Supreme Court in record time—less than a month after the first story appeared in the Times. The Court issued a terse, unsigned opinion rejecting the government's claim of authority to suppress the Pentagon Papers stories. Each Justice wrote a separate concurring or dissenting opinion in the case. Three Justices—Hugo L. Black, William

O. Douglas, and William J. Brennan, Jr.—argued that the government could never act to suppress such a story in a newspaper. Three Justices—Potter Stewart, Jr., Byron R. White, and Thurgood Marshall—maintained only that the government had not made a strong enough argument to justify suppressing newspaper stories in this case. And three Justices—the new Chief Justice and Justices John Marshall Harlan and Harry A. Blackmun—dissented, saying that the Pentagon Papers articles threatened the nation's security.

The retirements of Justices Black and Harlan in the summer of 1971 gave President Nixon two more chances to reshape the Court. He nominated a quiet, scholarly Virginian, Lewis F. Powell, Jr., and a brilliant, young, combative Justice Department lawyer, Assistant Attorney General William H. Rehnquist. Powell had no trouble winning Senate approval, but Rehnquist's road to the Court was rocky. Nevertheless, Rehnquist was confirmed. Rehnquist fulfilled the President's hopes that he would be a strict constructionist Justice, but Powell soon became one of the Court's pivotal members. He often decided cases by spelling out the competing interests at stake and then "balancing" them to decide which way he would vote.

In 1973, the Supreme Court tackled perhaps the most emotional and controversial constitutional issue since the Civil War: abortion. In the case of *Roe v. Wade*, a deeply divided Court ruled that in most circumstances, under the constitutional right of privacy identified and explained by the Warren Court, a woman has the right to control her body and to decide whether to go through with a pregnancy. The opinion, written by Justice Blackmun, struck its critics as more radical than anything the Warren Court had attempted. It was as far removed from "strict construction" as one could get. Over the years the Supreme Court has held firm, ruling again and again that *Roe v. Wade* is still good law and that the constitutional right of privacy exists even though the word does not specifically appear in the Constitution.

In 1974, to President Nixon's astonishment, *his* Supreme Court played a pivotal role in driving him from office. At issue were tape recordings of Presidential conversations in the Oval Office of the White House about the break-in at Democratic Party offices in the Washington, D.C., Watergate apartment complex by employees of President Nixon's re-election committee. A specially appointed federal prosecutor in the case claimed that the grand jury investigating the scandal needed the tape recordings to determine who should be indicted and brought to trial for federal crimes. The President replied that the principle of *executive privilege* required him to keep the tapes secret to preserve the aura of confidentiality that would enable Presidential advisers to give their real opinions without having to worry about disclosure and public reaction.

The Court voted, eight to zero, against the President. (Justice Rehnquist chose not to take part in the case because he had helped develop the President's argument for executive privilege when he was still at the Justice Department in the years before Watergate.) Chief Justice Burger, writing for the Court, agreed that executive privilege is part of our constitutional law. However, he ruled, it cannot stand as an absolute bar against the great public need for the administration of justice and the investigation of crimes. Burger ruled that, when a grand jury wanted Presidential tapes, documents, or testimony, and the President asserted executive privilege, the judge should be allowed to see or hear the material at issue in his or her own office—*in camera* is the Latin phrase lawyers use—and to decide which parts should be protected by executive privilege and which should be turned over to the court. This decision forced President Nixon to turn over tapes and transcripts that made his impeachment and removal from office a certainty. He resigned before the House of Representatives could impeach him.

Yet another great controversy arose during the era of the Burger Court. Many civil rights advocates believed that it was not enough just to say to black Americans, "You're equal now. Go compete." Black Americans labored under major disadvantages and needed special treatment to make their chances truly equal. Some scholars and public officials came up with an idea called *affirmative action*. Affirmative action permits admissions offices of colleges or graduate schools and government departments to give preference to qualified candidates who are also members of racial or ethnic minorities over qualified candidates who are not members of such minorities. Some other government officials came up with a different sort of plan—a *quota system* that sets aside a specific number of places for members of those minorities.

Allan Bakke, a white candidate for medical school, was turned down by the University of California at Davis even though he was qualified. All the places for non-minority-group students had been filled in the entering class, and Bakke, because he was white, was not allowed to claim one of the places held for minority-group students. He sued, claiming that his right to equal treatment under the Fourteenth Amendment and the federal civil rights laws had been violated by the UC-Davis plan.

The Supreme Court split badly again. Four Justices held that the Davis plan had violated the federal civil rights laws; Bakke should be admitted to the medical school for that reason only. Four Justices held that the Davis plan was not only legal but constitutional and that Bakke should lose. Justice Powell cast the deciding vote. He ruled that it was not enough to evaluate the UC-Davis plan under the federal civil rights laws—the question was whether the plan was constitutional. He then ruled that the UC-Davis plan was unconstitutional. Thus, he rejected the quota system. But he also ruled that an affirmative action plan *can* take race into account under the Constitution and the civil rights laws.

The affirmative action controversy continues to this day. Its opponents denounce it as "reverse discrimination"; its supporters claim that it is the only fair way to remedy centuries of racial and ethnic discrimination.

Chief Justice Burger stepped down in 1986 after seventeen years as Chief Justice during which he had worked hard to improve the quality and administration of the federal judicial system. He explained that he wanted to devote his energies to leading the national commission appointed to commemorate the bicentennial of the U.S. Constitution. (Chief Justice Burger shares a birthdate with the Constitution; its 200th birthday, on September 17, 1987, was his eightieth birthday.) Aside from judicial landmarks, his tenure as Chief Justice was notable because, in 1981, Sandra Day O'Connor became the first woman to be appointed to the Supreme Court. Justice O'Connor, who was a classmate of Justice Rehnquist at Stanford Law School, was appointed by President Ronald W. Reagan to succeed Justice Potter Stewart, who had retired.

There is as yet no clear legacy of the Burger Court. The Justices cut back on some major landmarks of the Warren era, such as the decisions outlining the doctrine of separation of church and state and restricting the use in criminal trials of evidence seized in violation of the Fourth Amendment. They built on and extended other Warren Court decisions, however, notably in the field of racial equality. In essence, the Burger Court was a period of marking time, of consolidating the bold advances of the Warren era, much as the Taney Court largely consolidated, developed, and preserved the experiments of the Marshall Court.

INTO THE THIRD CENTURY

To succeed Chief Justice Warren E. Burger, President Reagan named Justice William H. Rehnquist. Rehnquist ran into opposition from liberal Senators again but managed to win confirmation as the sixteenth Chief Justice. The Senate's vote to confirm—sixty-five to thirty-three—was the closest that any Chief Justice–designate has had since 1835, when the Senate confirmed Roger B. Taney (twenty-nine to fifteen). To fill the seat left vacant by Justice Rehnquist's promotion, President Reagan nominated and the Senate soon confirmed Judge Antonin Scalia, the first Italian-American to sit on the Court.

What will the Rehnquist Court bring? One indication may be the controversy stirred up by the announcement in the summer of 1987 that Justice Lewis F. Powell, Jr., would retire from the Court for reasons of poor health. Justice Powell had long been the "swing" vote on the Court. His position on constitutional issues was often critical in the many five-to-four decisions that the Burger Court handed down in the early 1980s.

President Reagan had long awaited the chance to appoint

COLLECTION OF THE SUPREME COURT OF THE UNITED STATES

*The Supreme Court, October Term, 1986: left to right, standing,
Sandra Day O'Connor (the first woman to sit on the Court),
Lewis F. Powell, Jr., John Paul Stevens, Antonin Scalia; left to
right, sitting, Thurgood Marshall, William J. Brennan, Jr., Chief
Justice William H. Rehnquist, Byron R. White, Harry A.
Blackmun. This was the Court several months before the
retirement of Justice Powell, who for nearly two decades was the
central figure in the Court's deciding of constitutional cases.*

a Justice who would tip the scales to a conservative jurisprudence more to his liking. His first choice to succeed Justice
Powell was a brilliant and combative former law professor,
Judge Robert H. Bork. Immediately, critics of the Bork
nomination organized to oppose his confirmation by the
Senate. Most observers doubted that Bork's opponents had a
chance to stop a nominee who was highly qualified to sit on
the Court and who was also the first choice of a powerful and
popular President.

Bork found his hearings before the Senate Judiciary Committee to be very rough going. In these televised sessions, he described for the Senators—and for the American people—his views on constitutional law. This was a major departure for a nominee. Previous nominees had declared that they could not talk about their views on constitutional law in any but the most general terms—dealing in specifics would compel them to prejudge issues that they might have to decide if they were confirmed. Bork took this step because he had written extensively about constitutional issues for law reviews and leading political magazines, and many Senators wanted to know if he still held the provocative opinions set forth in those articles. Judge Bork troubled moderate Senators because he seemed to backtrack on his views in order to persuade the Senate to vote to confirm him. This worry about "confirmation conversion," combined with both the Reagan Administration's surprisingly halfhearted efforts on Bork's behalf and the harsh and occasionally unfair anti-Bork campaign, led the Senate to reject Bork's nomination by a vote of fifty-six to forty-four, the largest vote to reject a nominee to the Court in American history.

The President cast about for another candidate. His second choice, Judge Douglas H. Ginsburg, seemed to many critics to be too inexperienced for elevation to the Supreme Court. The issue turned out to be moot. Judge Ginsburg withdrew his name under pressure from Reagan Administration officials after the news media reported that the nominee had smoked marijuana in violation of the law when he was a young professor at the Harvard Law School. (Ironically, it turned out that the Administration never formally submitted Judge Ginsburg's nomination to the full Senate.)

The President's third nominee, Judge Anthony M. Kennedy, had been frequently mentioned in the news media as a leading candidate for the Court. His views apparently echoed those of centrist Justice Powell. Judge Kennedy easily won unanimous confirmation by the Senate and became the 104th Justice, in February 1988.

As the Supreme Court completes its first two hundred years, it is a powerful and universally respected institution, however controversial specific decisions might be. Except for an occasional proposed constitutional amendment to overturn a specific decision by the Court, there is general agreement that the Court performs its duties and fulfills its responsibilities under the Constitution.

The only major controversy having to do with the structure of the federal judicial system revolves around the proposal to add a fourth level of federal courts between the present Courts of Appeals and the Supreme Court. Former Chief Justice Burger and several current Justices contend that the Supreme Court is badly overworked—that it cannot decide all the cases that it must decide. They want to create an *intercircuit tribunal,* a special court to which the Justices would refer cases in which different federal Courts of Appeals or state supreme courts dealing with federal issues have reached differing decisions on the same principle of law. The Supreme Court would review decisions of this intercircuit tribunal as a last resort, but the proposed new court would act as a safety valve to give the Justices more time to decide the cases that the Court should decide. Opponents of the idea claim that the new court would actually make more work for the Justices. In addition, a major study of the Court's workload conducted by New York University Law School indicates that the Court is not really overworked at all—thus striking a major blow at the case for the intercircuit tribunal.

The Court is the guardian of the Constitution—subject only to the decision by the people to adopt a constitutional amendment overturning a decision of the Justices. The Court's decisions on whether laws or other government actions are constitutional remind us at regular intervals of the values and principles at the core of the Constitution. The arguments before the Court, the briefs submitted to it, and the decisions and opinions handed down by the Justices are accessible to all. The Court also stands as the supervisor or manager of the federal judicial system, reaching out when it has to in order to promote coherence and consistency in federal law.

Justice Oliver Wendell Holmes, Jr., once wrote of the Court, "It is quiet here, but it is the quiet of a storm center." That is as true as ever as the Court enters its third century.

HOW THE SUPREME COURT
WORKS TODAY

In many ways, the U.S. Supreme Court is the most public of the three branches of government. This is how the Court does its job.

1. The Supreme Court chooses which cases it will hear. In nearly every instance, an individual or organization who wants the Court to hear his, her, or its case will file a *petition for a writ of certiorari*. This petition sets forth all the legal reasons for the Court to hear the case. The petition asks for a special document issued by the Court to the lower court saying, "Send the record of this case to us. We want to look it over." Whoever won in the decision of the lower court files a *brief in opposition*, a legal argument that the Court should *not* hear the case. The Justices read these petitions and briefs. Each Justice assigns one of his or her law clerks—top-ranked law school graduates who work for the Justice—to write reports on the petitions explaining the arguments and recommending which way the Justice should vote. Then the Justices meet in their conference room to vote. These sessions are private.

The Chief Justice has prepared a list, called the "discuss

list," of the cases that he thinks are important enough for the Justices to talk about. He speaks first, explaining each case and his reasoning about it. Each Justice then has a chance to speak, with the senior Justice going first and the newest Justice speaking last. Then they vote in reverse order, with the newest Justice voting first. If at least four Justices want to hear the case, the petition is granted. These votes are kept secret, but the announcements of which cases the Court accepts for review and which cases the Justices turn down are made public as soon as possible. Of about 2,000 to 3,000 cases the Court is asked to review each year, the Justices grant review in about 160 to 200. Sometimes several cases present the same questions. The Justices will put them together—a process that lawyers call *consolidating* cases for review.

2. At the next stage of the Court's work, the question is not whether the Justices should hear the case, but how they should rule on the issue the case presents. Lawyers call this stage *hearing the merits of the case*. Both sides file *briefs*—more legal arguments on the major issues in the case. The Justices and their clerks read these briefs carefully, as well as the documents setting forth the record of the case in the lower courts. Sets of briefs in each case are available in the Supreme Court Clerk's office for the news media, the legal community, and the public to read.

3. The Justices then listen to the lawyers for each side and other lawyers they sometimes invite to present arguments. These sessions, called *oral arguments*, are held in public. The Justices have the right to interrupt the lawyer who is arguing the case at any time to ask questions about the case. The lawyer is not there to make a speech, but to answer the Justices' questions. The best arguers, or *oral advocates*, know how to break their argument, answer the question, and finish a coherent presentation to the Court.

4. The Justices and their clerks consider what they have heard and read. In another conference, the Justices talk about

the case and then vote on it. If the Chief Justice is in the majority, he either decides to write the *opinion for the Court*—the essay explaining the Court's reasoning—or to assign it to another Justice. If there is a split, the Justices in the minority may write dissenting opinions. If the Chief Justice is in the minority, the Associate Justice who has been on the Court the longest assigns the writing of the opinion for the Court.

5. The Justices show one another drafts of their opinions. This stage of the process—*circulating opinions*—sometimes changes the ways that the Justices think about the case. The author of the opinion for the Court can answer points from the dissenting opinion or opinions in his or her draft. Sometimes a Justice in the majority likes the result but has different reasons for voting that way. He or she may write a concurring opinion explaining these different reasons. Sometimes a concurring opinion becomes the opinion for the Court as Justices change their minds and votes. Sometimes a dissent can become the opinion for the Court, and the draft opinion for the Court can become a dissent. This whole process is secret.

6. On the days that the Court announces its decisions, the Justices meet the press and the public in the Supreme Court chamber, and the decisions for each day are read out one by one. The Supreme Court print shop has already printed up copies of the opinions for distribution at that time to the winning and losing sides and to the news media. Special newsletters for lawyers and law professors publish the opinions in full. Eventually, unofficial series of reports issued by law book companies and the official *United States Reports* publish the Court's decisions for all to read. Law professors and students write articles in magazines called *law reviews* analyzing the Court's decisions and opinions, offering praise or criticism. The process of developing our constitutional law continues until the next round of cases.

FOR FURTHER READING

(An asterisk indicates that a paperback edition is available.)

The best introduction to the Constitution's principles and history is John Sexton and Nat Brandt, *How Free Are We? What the Constitution Says We Can and Cannot Do* (New York: M. Evans, 1986)*; a more unconventional and very popular treatment is Jerome Agel and Mort Gerberg, *The U.S. Constitution for Everyone* (New York: Perigee/Putnam, 1987)*. An excellent short general history of the United States is Allan Nevins and Henry Steele Commager, *A Pocket History of the United States*, 7th ed. (New York: Pocket Books, 1987)*. The best single-volume constitutional history of the United States is Alfred H. Kelly, Winfred A. Harbison, and Herman Belz, *The American Constitution: Its Origins and Development*, 6th ed. (New York: Norton, 1983). The best study of the Federal Convention of 1787 is Clinton L. Rossiter, *1787: The Grand Convention* (New York: Norton, 1987)*. Richard B. Bernstein with Kym S. Rice, *Are We to Be a Nation? The Making of the Constitution* (Cambridge, Mass.: Harvard University Press, 1987)*, presents an overview of the era of the American Revolution based on the latest scholarship.

Robert G. McCloskey, *The American Supreme Court* (Chicago: University of Chicago Press, 1960)*, is a classic treatment in great need of updating. A far more recent study, and one of very high quality, is William M. Wiecek, *Liberty Under Law* (Baltimore: Johns Hopkins University Press, 1988)*. Three brief and graceful studies by Archibald Cox also stand out: *The Warren Court* (Cambridge, Mass.: Harvard University Press, 1968)*; *The Role of the Supreme Court in American Government* (New York: Oxford University Press, 1976)*; and *Freedom of Expression* (Cambridge, Mass.: Harvard University Press, 1981)*. Professor Cox's more general study, *The Court and the Constitution* (Boston: Houghton Mifflin, 1987), builds on his earlier works. It is also a good introduction to the more theoretical side of constitutional law.

Of the many histories of leading constitutional cases, the best are: Don E. Fehrenbacher, *The Dred Scott Case* (New York: Oxford University Press, 1978), also in an abridged edition, *Slavery, Law, and Politics* (New York: Oxford University Press, 1981)*; Richard Kluger, *Simple Justice* (New York: Alfred A. Knopf, 1976)*; and Anthony M. Lewis, *Gideon's Trumpet* (New York: Random House, 1964)*.

INDEX